Praise for *Look Both Ways* . . .

"With so many professing to understand how Internet sexual predators operate online, finding the real experts is a challenge. I look no further than Linda Criddle. She is one of the few people in the field I turn to with questions—a mom, a child protection advocate, and a friend. Children are safer because of her caring and work."

Parry Aftab
Internet Privacy and Security Lawyer
and Executive Director of WiredSafety.org

"As an Internet child safety expert at Microsoft, Linda has an impressive background in online child protection, dealing with predatory behavior and in product risk analysis. Her work as an investigative journalist has honed a sharp, incisive, and methodical mind, which expresses itself in highly accessible writing. Being herself a mother of four also means Linda is always grounded in the nitty gritty realities of every parent's daily struggle to do the best they can for their kids."

John Carr
Chair of the UK's Children's Charities'
Coalition on Internet Safety

*"*Look Both Ways *is both informative and a much needed resource for a range of audiences, including business, government, parents, teachers, and even perhaps young people themselves. Whilst much is said about the risks to children online, there is little commentary that articulates them clearly and then goes on to identify ways in which they can be managed in a proactive and meaningful way.* Look Both Ways *will have significant international value, especially for those tasked with making the online world safer for children."*

Annie Mullins
Vodafone Global Content Standards Manager

"Once upon a time, the most serious concern a parent would have about the media life of a young child was whether a TV show was on too late in the evening. Things have surely changed. In today's world of blogs, downloads, and the Internet, parents need to be armed with every tool available as well as their own good judgment. And parents must take proactive steps toward ensuring their child's safety. In Look Both Ways, *Linda Criddle provides those tools and gives the very clear message that parents must do what others either will not, or can not, do—protect their children from the insidious forces that are ready to take advantage."*

Neil J. Salkind, Ph.D.
University of Kansas

Microsoft®

Look Both Ways: Help Protect Your Family on the Internet

Linda Criddle
with Nancy Muir

PUBLISHED BY
Microsoft Press
A Division of Microsoft Corporation
One Microsoft Way
Redmond, Washington 98052-6399

Library of Congress Control Number: 2006927199
978-0-7356-2347-7
0-7356-2347-3

Printed and bound in the United States of America.

1 2 3 4 5 6 7 8 9   QWE   1 0 9 8 7 6

Distributed in Canada by H.B. Fenn and Company Ltd.

A CIP catalogue record for this book is available from the British Library.

Microsoft Press books are available through booksellers and distributors worldwide. For further information about international editions, contact your local Microsoft Corporation office or contact Microsoft Press International directly at fax (425) 936-7329. Visit our Web site at www.microsoft.com/mspress. Send comments to mspinput@microsoft.com.

Acquisitions Editor: Juliana Aldous Atkinson
Developmental Editor: Sandra Haynes
Project Editor: Melissa von Tschudi-Sutton
Artist: Jessie Good
Project Management: Publishing.com
Compositor: Curtis Philips
Copy Editor and Proofreader: Andrea Fox
Indexer: Wright Information Indexing Services
Design: Happenstance, Maureen Forys

Body Part No. X12-64008

This book is dedicated to you, the Internet generation,
whether you are navigating the Web for yourself
or as parents valiantly trying to provide
a safe and nurturing environment for your family.

Acknowledgments

The inspiration for this book came from you. Your requests for more information in a format you could take away and share with others led me to Bill Shaughnessy's office with the suggestion of writing a book. Bill, and my manager Jeff Dossett, wholeheartedly encouraged me, and I've yet to decide whether to thank or curse them for that backing, as I truly did not know how much work this would be.

I'm privileged to have been under the tutelage of so many veterans in the book industry. I owe a profound debt to Nancy Muir whose coauthoring and (firm) guidance have been invaluable. She's become a wonderful mentor and friend. Deep gratitude also goes to the Microsoft Press team: to Juliana Aldous and Lucinda Rowley who read the proposal and believed this book would be important; to Melissa von Tschudi-Sutton whose unflagging labor kept all the parts moving forward in the kindest way; to Sandra Haynes for her lost weekends; to Chris Nelson who gracefully assuaged issues that arose; and to Jessie Good, Curtis Philips, Andrea Fox, and Jan Wright, who all contributed to this final product. I am grateful for the care each of you invested in the development of this book.

I also want to thank those who read chapters, provided feedback, and improved this book with your insights, including my parents Richard and JoAn Criddle, David Milstein, Alan Packer, Michael Aldridge, Brian Holdsworth, Amie Servais, Chris Martenson, and Jerry Johnson.

I'm extremely beholden to Ernie Allen, President and CEO, National Center for Missing & Exploited Children (NCMEC); John Carr, Chair of the UK's Children's Charities' Coalition on Internet Safety; Annie Mullins, Vodafone Global Content Standards Manager; Parry Aftab, Internet Privacy and Security Lawyer and Executive Director of wiredsafety.org; Lucy Berliner, Director, Harborview Center for Sexual Assault and Traumatic Stress, and Clinical Associate Professor, University of Washington School of Social Work and Department of Psychiatry and Behavioral Sciences; Kenneth V. Lanning, former Supervisory Special Agent and profiler with the FBI; and Neil J. Salkind, PhD in Psychology and Education Research; all have reviewed portions of the book and/or generously provided quotes.

Special acknowledgment goes to those who graciously let me tell their stories or use their photos, and who will remain nameless for safety reasons, but far from forgotten.

I'd like to express particular appreciation for those closest to me: my youngest son who unselfishly tolerated my long hours at the computer; my older children and parents for their encouragement and belief in me; the loony ladies' club who've been my safety net; my wonderful friends who have always helped me along the way.

And to David, whose support never fails me.

Finally, I'm grateful to everyone who has supported and encouraged this book, because *Internet safety is everyone's responsibility.*

Table of Contents

Introduction

Buy a newspaper today, and odds are you'll find a story about online abuses: a public figure arrested for soliciting a child online . . . a teenager assaulted by somebody he met in a chat room . . . identity theft made possible by poor safety procedures in a large company . . . e-mail fraud being perpetrated on the public in staggering numbers . . . or a new destructive computer virus.

The Internet has quickly become an integral part of society. Businesses, schools, media, and communication with others all are highly dependent on opportunities the Internet has created. Unfortunately, it is not only "good" people and businesses that are leveraging these new technologies.

The rash of criminal misuses of the Internet reported in the news leaves many feeling like they should prevent their children from using the Web at all, quit banking or shopping online, and regard e-mail messages as potentially threatening. You're left with a general feeling of vulnerability and helplessness. When you can't even see online criminals coming, how can you protect yourself from them?

Avoiding the Internet isn't a very practical solution. While there are legitimate reasons for concern, there is *much* you can do to become more empowered and start using the Internet on *your terms*. That's what this book is all about.

Is This Book for You?

If you use the Internet, this book is for you. You don't have to be a teen blogger or even have children. You can be any age at all. You don't have to be a techie type. In fact, if you have a fear of technology and you want to use the Internet, this book should help to reassure you that protecting yourself online doesn't require a degree in technology—it requires a change in your behavior. If you consider yourself a technical person, you need the skills presented in this book as much as the least technical person does.

If you want to take steps to ensure that you and your family are safer while browsing, shopping, communicating, and interacting online, this book will help you create the infrastructure necessary to do that.

Start with a Technology Base

You absolutely must protect your devices from attacks via spam, viruses, spyware, Trojan horses, worms, and so on, and there are plenty of books that will tell you how to do that. Although we provide a "Technology Toolkit" section (see Part Four of this book) that outlines some basic tools that you will find useful, technology is not the focus of this book.

This book is intended to help you and your family be safer *after* those protections are in place because technical protections alone are not enough. Those protections guard against software attacks. This book will help you *learn how to guard against the human predators roaming the Internet.*

Think about it this way: You put protections into your home to help keep you safe from intruders. You install locks on windows and doors, set up outdoor lighting, and perhaps even use motion detectors and a security system. These can help to keep you safe. But all of these precautions don't help at all if a stranger is able to talk his way into your home, or if you hand over your credit card or bank account number to a stranger online.

How This Book Is Organized

To help you understand the current status of the Internet environment, the risks that can affect everyone, and how to become safer online almost immediately, this book first provides a checklist of steps you can take to become safer today and is then divided into four parts.

Part One provides an overview of the types of activity going on today that can put you and your family at risk online. Chapter 1 explores how the same types of crimes that occur offline are now being committed online, only with different tools. Chapter 2 explores many of the misconceptions about anonymity online that can lull many people into behaving differently than they would in a face-to-face situation and putting themselves at risk. Finally, Chapter 3 looks at some typical traits and behaviors of online predators so that you can understand the motivations and methods of these people and better protect yourself against them.

Part Two comprises 13 chapters that offer simple steps you can take right now to be safer online. Each of these chapters offers a fictionalized example of risky behavior, an analysis of that behavior, an overview of the broader risks, and advice for protecting yourself.

In Part Three, the focus is on the action plans you can put in place to better protect your family, starting today. For example, Chapter 17 provides a discussion guide you can use to begin the dialog with your family and friends about creating a plan to help keep all of you safer online. Chapter 18 offers resources and advice for how to report abuses you encounter and how to work to effect legislation; this chapter also provides information about some different grassroots efforts to improve online safety for everybody, worldwide.

Part Four provides valuable resources for you. It includes

- A glossary of terms to help you stay on top of the abundance of technical and social networking terminology that is quickly becoming part of your vocabulary. Each glossary term appears in **bold** the first time it's used in the book.

- Information about the basic technology tools you should put to work to protect your computer and filter access to content, if you want to do so.

- A list of valuable Web resources for information about online safety and reporting abuses.

- A list of common abbreviations used in e-mail, instant messaging, and text messaging.

Special Elements

Throughout the book, you'll notice special elements that are worth mentioning, including:

- **Find Out More**   These are tips about where you can get more information about a topic, either in another chapter of this book, or from a Web site or organization.

- **Think About It**   These offer ideas that might intrigue you or challenge the way you think about online safety. They also make interesting kick-off questions for discussions with family and friends on a specific topic.

- **Sidebars** These provide background information or more in-depth data about a topic in the chapter.

How to Get the Most from This Book

This book provides many specific actions you can take to protect yourself and your family online. By simply reading this book, you will gain a much better understanding of the types of threats that exist online and what you can do to make you safer than you are today, immediately.

The best way to use this book is to first read it cover to cover. For the most part, you will quickly understand the principles because I relate them to common situations in your everyday life. Absorb the main messages, and then go back and focus on the possible areas of risk one by one. If you use e-mail frequently, go back to the e-mail chapter and pick the suggestions that work for you. If your child wants to start an online journal (called a blog), go back to that chapter and review my advice. Not all advice will work for every individual or family; choose the suggestions that are right for you.

Don't try to absorb every tip and suggestion I provide the first time out. Remember the first time you got behind the wheel of a car? You were probably nervous and didn't think you could ever deal with all the sensory input that came at you as you drove that first tentative block. You might read this book and feel a similar sensory overload. But give yourself time and implement the advice bit by bit, and you'll feel more comfortable implementing the advice that applies to your situation in short order.

The Internet provides a lot of opportunity for sharing, communicating, commerce, and entertainment. By educating yourself about how to use it in a safer way, you can feel more confident enjoying all the advantages it has to offer.

In addition to this book, I've created a Web site at *www.look-both-ways. com*. It provides additional material and links to help you in your efforts to become safer online. On this Web site, you'll find additional examples you can use to practice with; templates for negotiating safety expectations with others; recent news articles that might be of interest; top safety tips for different types of online products and services; overviews of new Internet features as they're developed; an update on emerging online safety issues and ongoing tips to help you stay safe; and links to other resources. The site also includes a way for you to ask questions about Internet safety that you might still have or that might come up in the future. I will try to respond to your questions as quickly as possible and make the questions and answers available for everyone to learn from.

Note

Though the material presented is based on true examples, at the time of the printing of this book, all example companies, organizations, products, domain names, e-mail addresses, blog handles, blog sites, depictions of IM chat sessions, e-mail message examples, Web site examples, logos, people, places, and events described or illustrated herein were fictitious or were owned by the author. No association with any real company, organization, blog site or handle, Web site, domain name, e-mail address, IM session, logo, person, place, or event is intended or should be inferred.

Quick Safety Checklist

Every chapter in this book is packed with lists of advice, which can seem overwhelming at first glance. To help you focus on the most important actions to take today to improve your online safety, I have provided this checklist.

Here are the top 13 things you can do today to become safer online:

1. **Buy all the safety software you need** for your devices, and use good filtering software. Keep them current and use them unfailingly. This should be as automatic as locking your door when you leave the house. *Also see "Technology Toolkit."*

2. **Sit down and discuss online safety and come to an agreement with your family and friends.** Set rules about how you will protect each other online. Don't blame, don't accuse, and don't run scared; simply set some logical parameters to what activities are okay and what information can be exposed online and with whom. These rules need to reflect your personal and family values. *Also see Chapter 17.*

3. **Be conscious and selective about who you interact with online.** Dealing with people you know, your family, and friends has relatively low risk. Going into public chat rooms, opening your blog up to the general public, and posting information in other public venues increases the risk significantly. *Also see Chapter 4.*

4. **Be sensitive about what you're putting online that's accessible to the public,** including anything that can personally identify you or someone else: unaltered photos of yourself or information in your profile such as your birth date, town, e-mail address, school name, and so on. These can be used to locate you or steal your identity. *Also see Chapters 4 and 5.*

5. **Be cautious about e-mail.** Don't open e-mail from people you don't know or open attachments unless you verify that somebody you

know sent them to you. Never respond to e-mail asking you to provide personal information, especially your account number or password, even if it seems to be from somebody you do business with. Your bank (or any other reputable business) should not ask you for this information in an e-mail message. *Also see Chapter 10.*

6. **Put your family computer and any game consoles that connect to the Internet in a public room** where you can monitor your children's online activity. *Also see Chapter 13.*

7. **Never, ever meet somebody you've met online in person without taking somebody else along.** Remember, people are not always who they seem to be online. More than 90 percent of kids who meet an online predator in person end up being abused (Wolak et al., 2004). *Also see Chapter 3.*

8. **Review the features your children have on mobile phones** that they carry with them all day. Can they download images from the Internet, instant message with people, or access location services that allow others to pinpoint their location? All of these features could be a cause for concern, depending on your child's maturity and situation. *Also see Chapter 15.*

9. **Inform yourself about how and where to report abuses** and create an environment that encourages your kids to report abuse to you. By acting as a responsible Internet citizen, you can help stop the illegal activity, harassment, and predatory behavior of the criminal population online. *Also see Chapter 18.*

10. **Don't let yourself or your kids trade personal information to get so-called freebies.** Just as in the physical world, if it sounds too good to be true, it probably is. *Also see Chapter 14.*

11. **Familiarize yourself with the Internet safety rules being applied in your children's schools and at their friends' houses,** because they might be logging on from these other locations. *Also see Chapters 12, 17, and 18.*

12. **Don't use e-mail addresses, IM names, chat nicknames, and so on that give away too much personal information.** Make them gender-neutral, with no age or location information, and do not make them sound provocative. *Also see Chapter 5.*

13. **Sit down with your child and review buddies, blogs, browser history, image files, music downloads, and so on.** Let them know you'll do this periodically. Explain that this is not to violate their privacy, but to protect them and the family from risks. *Also see Chapter 17.*

PART ONE

Understanding the Risks

CHAPTER ONE

The Landscape of Risk

Marty's feeling good tonight; his law firm just won a big case, and it's a sure bet he'll make partner before his 45th birthday next month. He checks on his wife, and she's watching TV in the living room, starting to doze. He grabs a drink and settles down in front of his computer in the den. Marty logs on to the Internet, turns off the computer speakers so his wife won't hear anything, and types in a **URL***.*

Marty discovered Stella a couple of months ago. She's 14 and lives in a nearby city. Like most people, her online journal, called a **blog***, tells more about her than she realizes, and, like most blogs, it was set up by default to be wide open to the public. In her blog profile she lists her birthday, city and state, her favorite movies, and favorite color. Her blog name is 2SexyStella, and the picture she's posted on her blog space is that of a slim young girl with big eyes, tight jeans and halter top, and the slouching posture of a teen who is unsure of herself and self-conscious, but trying hard to look cool.*

When he first came across Stella's blog, Marty was attracted to her photo, so he started checking her Web site regularly. When Stella posted a complaint about having an argument with her mother, Marty saw the opening he'd been waiting for. He posted a sympathetic and supportive response. He sided with Stella against her mom, introducing a wedge between them, and slowly taking on a role as a confidante. After a few more exchanges through her blog, Stella gave him her e-mail address. They've been e-mailing and **instant messaging** *each other for weeks now. It never ceases to amaze Marty how* *much information people provide about themselves, their family, and their friends without even realizing it.*

For her part, Stella was thrilled to find that Marty was so cute, and only a few years older than her. He thinks she's the most wonderful person alive. They have so much in common! They love the same movies and even share the same birthday. They've swapped pictures of their families and houses. (Stella never realized the photo of her sitting on her front porch contained the house number and a street sign in the background, so now he knows where she lives.) She's just excited by how this 17-year-old guy flirts with her.

In his last e-mail, Marty asked if Stella had a digital camera, and they began sharing personal photos using instant messaging. The first picture he asked for was innocent, but now that he's established the connection, who knows where this friendship could go?

What's Going On Out There?

There was a time when you had to leave your house to shop, hang out with friends, visit the library, or meet a date. That's changed: Now you can do all this and much more online. The Internet has enabled fantastic opportunities for education, social contact, and entertainment, and it enriches hundreds of millions of lives every day. For most people, most of the time, that convenience is a tremendous asset and the Web is a powerful tool. But just as there are potential dangers any time you get into your car and drive across town, there are potential dangers on the Web.

What the Internet does for "good" people, it also does for "bad" people: It gives broad access to people and information and allows users to remain largely anonymous. Criminals leverage any tool they can to commit their crimes; their latest tool of choice is the Internet. Often referred to as **cybercriminals** or predators, these individuals are committing a wide variety of offenses from **identity theft** and harassment to stalking and assault. Is what's going on all that different from what criminals have done for years and what you've learned to protect yourself from offline? No. Only the tools at their disposal have changed.

That there are bad people out there is a fact of life, but the existence of cybercriminals should not force you to avoid the Internet any more than you avoid walking or driving because a bad driver might do you harm. You walk down the street without fear because you learned as a child to *look both ways* and cross streets safely. The same is true for the Internet. You can use this powerful tool safely if you understand not only the opportunities the Web provides, but also the risks and what you can do to mitigate those risks. Then you can make choices that provide the level of protection you want for yourself and your family.

Who Are These Cybercriminals?

If you have a particular image of the type of person who commits these types of crimes, it's probably wrong. **Predators** come in every age, shape, and gender and live in any part of the world:

- Many are well-respected business or professional people who appear to be upstanding citizens.

- Sexual predators who target minors are predominantly, though not exclusively, male (95 percent; Wolak et al., 2004).

- Predators might act alone, in loose groups, or in formal gangs. Even organized crime syndicates are cashing in on people's online vulnerabilities.

- There is also a "middleman" predator class out there, assembling publicly available information into virtual catalogs and selling that information to anybody willing to pay. Some of these catalogs contain mundane information such as your preference in soft drinks and TV programs, but other catalogs list your identity, home address, age, photos, and other identifying information.

Find Out More

For more detail about who predators are and their behavior, see Chapter 3, "Thinking Like the Enemy: Predatory Behavior."

Who's Vulnerable?

Who could become an online victim? Quite simply, anybody. Whether you go online yourself or another person or company puts information about you online, there are risks. Depending on the type of information out there, your risk might be fairly low or significant. Children are at special risk because of their high volume of online activity and naïveté about human nature. However, people of all ages, even those who make their livings in law enforcement and computer security, are astounded when I point out what information is being shared online and with what consequences.

> **Think About It**
>
> The most critical years for children are around ages 13 to 15, when they begin to reach out and form relationships with others. These kids are often not streetwise, and they are looking for validation and approval, rebelling against their parents' values, and drawn to the latest technologies. They are discovering who they are and enjoy trying on other identities. Online predators know this and take full advantage of it (Wolak et al., 2004).

But, you say, you use **antivirus software**. You regularly scan to rid your computer of **spyware**, and you turned on your computer **firewall**. You even have **content filtering** installed to try to prevent your kids from viewing pornography. But consider this: *It's not just about technology; it's about your online behavior.*

A firewall is useless against financial fraud. If your elderly mother willingly responds to an e-mail purporting to be from her insurance company, asking her to provide her bank account information for a direct deposit of a refund, all the software in the world won't help. There's no antivirus program on the planet that will protect your daughter if she posts messages on her blog that give away her location, her age, and her vulnerable emotions.

> **Think About It**
>
> Once you have technical protections in place, you might well be the biggest remaining risk factor. But because your behavior is in your control, you can feel empowered to reduce your risk online.

How Big Is the Problem?

The Internet provides unparalleled opportunities for instant access to information and helpful services. Unfortunately, cybercriminals are among the most adept at leveraging these new technologies, and have embraced the Internet to facilitate their criminal behavior.

When you include cell phone Internet services, there are over 2 billion people worldwide with Internet access. Within the United States alone, there are over 21 million kids online, according to the Pew Internet & American Life Project. Cybercriminals are keenly aware of the opportunity and are targeting these groups accordingly.

The magnitude of the abuse problem is proportional to the number of potential victims. Consider that

- In Canada, 94 percent of kids report they have Internet access from home (Media Awareness Network, 2005). In the United Kingdom, 90 percent of children have a personal computer at home, and 75 percent have Internet access (*www.childwise.co.uk*).

- A 2004 study by the National Cyber Security Alliance and America Online found that 80 percent of home computers are infected with spyware or **adware**, and 63 percent of users have encountered a computer **virus.**

- In 2005, the worldwide financial impact of **malware** (virus, spyware, and so on) attacks was $14.2 billion, according to *www.computereconomics.com*.

- Testimony given before a U.S. congressional panel (April 2006) noted that commercial child pornography on the Internet worldwide in 2005 was a $20 billion business. The trade in child pornography in the United States alone is estimated at approximately $3 billion.

- 12 percent of Web sites include pornography, and 25 percent of **search engine** requests are for pornography, according to *www.familysafemedia.com*.

- One in five children ages 12 to 17 are sexually solicited online every year in the United States (according to the National Center for Missing and Exploited Children, NCMEC), and a similar number is estimated in the United Kingdom (according to the Internet Crime Forum).

- In the year 2000 there was an average of 220 arrests a month for Internet sex crimes against minors in the United States (Wolak et al., 2003). But the problem is worldwide: Law enforcement agencies around the world are expanding their online criminal units to combat the growth of online crime.

- One account of a teenage boy who sold sexual images of himself via webcam reported that he had 1,500 customers. The majority of these were professionals such as doctors, lawyers, businesspeople, and teachers.

How Are You Putting Yourself at Risk?

You are in danger on the Internet from two directions: inbound and outbound (see Figure 1-1). Spam, viruses, and spyware flow toward you through e-mail, instant messaging (IM), Web sites, and so on. They can be downloaded onto your computer without your knowledge. There is much you can do to protect yourself from these threats, and most online security books focus on this kind of defense. (See "Technology Toolkit" in Part Four for my basic advice about implementing technical protections.)

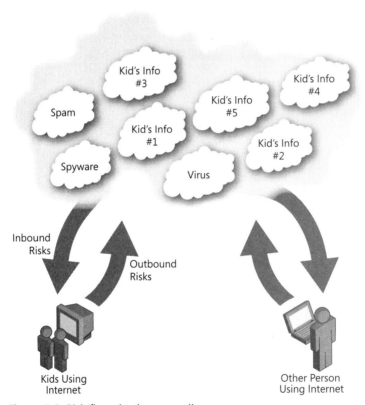

Figure 1-1 Risk flows both ways online.

Perhaps more dangerous are outbound risks; these occur when you willingly (though often unwittingly) reveal information about yourself through the data you put online every day. You might be providing the very information cybercriminals need to take advantage of you. Outbound risk is the focus of this book.

One of the most important things you can do to reduce your own vulnerability is to grasp this one concept: Every piece of information about you is a valuable commodity. Publically available user information has the potential to be tracked, cataloged, analyzed, and sold, both legally and illegally.

The fact is that many people, particularly but certainly not exclusively children, are making available a variety of information via the Web that makes them identifiable and places them at risk every day.

Find Out More

For more about how to avoid giving away too much information about yourself, see Chapter 5, "Step 2: Don't Tell People More Than You Should."

What kind of information are people putting out there? I'm not talking about your bank account or social security number—you wouldn't deliberately give those to strangers any more than you would hand somebody your wallet. I'm talking about seemingly useless information about you, from your favorite book to your age, the color of your eyes, and even what makes you sad or happy. Using that information and a few facts about you, such as your name and address, a predator can find you and use key information about you to either impersonate you, steal from you, or initiate a relationship.

Think about what you or your friends have shared online about you, and the people out there who might use that personal information to impersonate or approach you, and then consider these statistics:

- 67 percent of teen bloggers provide their age; 54 percent provide specific demographic information; 61 percent provide contact information; and 39 percent include their birth date (Huffaker et al., 2005).

- 76 percent of victims of online sexual exploitation are found via **social networking** applications such as **chat rooms, discussion boards**, and blogs (Wolak et al., 2004).

- 63 percent of all bloggers use **emoticons** (little icons that show their emotional state) (Huffaker et al., 2005).

- Approximately 50 percent of people blogging are doing so as a form of self-therapy (The AOL Blog Trends Survey. Digital Marketing

Services, Inc., 2005). (This means that they are emotionally vulnerable and might reveal more than they should about themselves.)

Remember that you control the level of your exposure through the information you place online. Risk is commensurate with the choices you make about the type of content you post, the breadth of contacts you make information available to, and whether you share information about others as well as yourself. The more personal the information you choose to share, the more careful you should be to share only with close friends and family (see Figure 1-2).

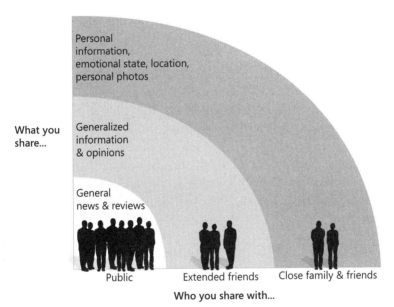

Figure 1-2 The amount you share online should be determined by your intended audience.

Think About It

Sit down and make a list of all the information about you that might interest a cyber-criminal. Check off the items you've made available online in any fashion. Search on your name to see what information you can find. When you go online, think about exactly what you want to share with total strangers, and what you want to reserve for more trusted groups of people.

What Can You Do?

So, what's the answer to avoiding risk? Do you disconnect your computer, cancel your Internet service, and hide under your bed, safe from all that online danger? Of course not. Just as your parents taught you to be careful when you walk around town, to obey the school crossing guard and look both ways before crossing a street, you simply need to learn how to look both ways when you move around the Web.

Think of it this way: Cars, buses, and trucks are wonderful tools, but they can be dangerous in certain circumstances. According to the Department of Transportation, in the United States alone, over 40,000 people die every year in traffic accidents. To mitigate the risks, you teach your children about traffic safety. You don't avoid walking across the street for fear of all the danger out there because you know the rules and how to protect yourself.

Making the Internet Safer for Your Family

The Internet is also a wonderful tool, offering a vibrant world of interaction and information. The problem is that nobody taught you or your children how to be online safely because the entire online world didn't even exist in its current state 10 years ago. That lack of training has left you and your family open to a variety of risks online. Fortunately, these risks can be minimized by taking a few easy steps.

I wrote this book to give you some of the tools you need to act safely on the Web and take advantage of all the positive things it has to offer without fear. Some of these tools involve technology. The good news is that, more and more, safety measures are being built into the software you use every day—your operating system and browser, for instance. There are good tools out there and you should use them. But remember: The most important step you can take, starting today, is to educate yourself and your family about the risks and make informed choices about your online behavior.

Taking the First Step

I won't tell you to never post a picture online, to dismantle your blog, or to never have an online date; that type of advice makes about as much sense as telling you to never leave your house or never cross a street to avoid being hit by a car. What I will teach you is how to recognize some common risks and predatory behavior, how to come to an educated decision about your personal risk tolerance and comfort zone, and how to define a framework for online interactions for you and your family.

If you're a parent, you have to move beyond the idea that Internet security is something you can "do" to your kids by following them around online. Just as you can't follow your kids all around town during the day, you can't be there every minute they spend online. Instead, with a few simple steps you and your family can learn how to protect yourselves with a three-tiered approach of education, infrastructure, and enforcement.

When cars came into peoples' lives, society had to do that same thing. People *educated* themselves about how to drive and cross streets safely, they created an *infrastructure* of roads, sidewalks, street signs, and regulations to keep drivers and pedestrians safe, and they *enforced* those regulations. That same approach is necessary when you drive around online. For the time being, however, that education, infrastructure, and enforcement might rest mainly in your own hands as schools and government scramble to come up with solutions and put them in place.

Find Out More

See Chapters 17, "Talking About Safety," and 18, "It Takes Everyone to Make a Safe Internet," for more about how to implement this three-tiered approach in your family.

You Are Not Alone

Internet companies and regulatory authorities are becoming much more aware of the problem and are taking action. Companies are investing in online safety. Laws have been created to facilitate the prosecution of a wide variety of online crimes.

As this book goes to press, the U.S. House of Representatives is holding hearings on the sexual exploitation of children, and there are several Internet safety proposals up for consideration. Funding for the Justice Department Internet Crimes Against Children (ICAC) program jumped from $2.4 million in 1998 to $14.5 million in 2005.

In France, a law has been passed requiring all Internet service providers to provide content filtering features. Governments around the world are mobilizing to provide educational materials and regulatory infrastructure. The United Kingdom has established a crime unit, CEOP, to target online child sexual predators. The Royal Canadian Mounted Police and Microsoft have jointly developed a tracking system (Child Exploitation

Tracking System, or CETS) to facilitate the discovery and prosecution of child sexual predators. Australia has established a safe ISP program called Ladybird, and similar programs are being created around the world.

The news is hopeful for a better Internet in years to come. But the strongest link in online safety today is you.

What's Next?

The 13 chapters in Part Two of this book provide 13 simple steps you can take to protect yourself and your family. Part Three gives you advice on putting those steps into action.

Just as you learned to look both ways as you were crossing the street when you were young, you can learn to look both ways and use the Internet more safely, without fear.

CHAPTER TWO

Misperceptions About Online Anonymity

One of the big attractions of the Internet for many people is the anonymity they believe it affords. They can go where they like, say what they like, even pretend to be anyone they like, and nobody will be the wiser. Unfortunately, that sense of anonymity and the security it provides is often false. You might believe you are anonymous when you post a message in a discussion forum, on a publicly accessible blog, in a chat room, or on a social networking site, but most people do a poor job of maintaining anonymity. As a result, all too many Internet users are operating under a false sense of security.

Remember that the ability to remain anonymous works two ways. Potential **scam** artists, criminals, or predators **surfing** the Internet also have the benefit of anonymity; however, unlike the average user, they are often very skilled at maintaining their anonymity and take great care to do so. They are frequently very skilled in creating false personalities that help them perpetrate whatever kind of crime they want to commit: conning users in a financial fraud, stealing identities, or targeting children.

Leaving a Trail of Clues

Who poses the greatest threat to your anonymity online? In most cases, it's probably you, a family member, or a close friend. The fact that it's not some faceless stranger putting your information out there is good news, because it means that by learning a few simple guidelines, you can have more control over some of the information that might appear online.

You often unknowingly leak valuable clues to your identity through a wide variety of actions. For example, an e-mail address might clearly identify you, allowing those lurking online to find you with no sophisticated hacking required. Peter15surfer@theReef.au provides a name, an age, a hobby to help strike up a conversation, and the fact that he lives near the Great Barrier Reef in Australia. For someone targeting a certain demographic, this would be enough to get their attention.

This trail of clues is not limited to your Internet activities on your computer. Consider, for example, that if you send a **text message** from your cell phone, your phone number is included with the message as part of the address. You or your child might think you are keeping your identity, location, or contact information safe when you're text messaging someone you don't know or trust, but in reality you are broadcasting valuable information to everyone who sees the message.

Posting information that is available only to close friends or family doesn't pose an increased threat because they already know where you live, what you look like, and how to contact you. On the other hand, your anonymity is at risk any time you post personally identifiable information (often referred to as PII) such as your name, address, or photo, or whenever you post indirectly identifiable information such as the name of your school, your street, or your sports team in an online forum available to the general public. Cybercriminals can collect these pieces of information to discern your location, habits, interests, age, and more.

What can somebody do with that information? The answer is *anything they want*. They might sell it to others, steal your identity, commit fraud and ruin your credit, come to your house and rob it, or attempt to assault you or your child, for example.

Find Out More

See Chapter 4, "Step 1: Be Careful What You Show People," for more about how and where you might be inadvertently revealing information about yourself through photos, videos, and other visual clues.

The Lure of Anonymity

The irony is that because most people feel that nobody knows who they are online, they often become more forthcoming about themselves in a very public way. They feel liberated, telling total strangers things that they might not tell those they know well. They end up giving away a tremendous amount of information that criminals can use to take advantage of them. Children who find it hard to talk to parents or friends about sensitive subjects might be most at risk by placing their trust in online strangers.

Consider a teenager who joins a chat or creates a blog. He might find the sympathy he gets from an online "friend" refreshing after what seems like a lack of understanding from his parents or peers. Predators are masters at gaining trust, using the shield of online anonymity to their advantage by appearing to be something or someone they are not.

How Predators Use Anonymity

Because online cybercriminals know very well how to hide their identities and intentions, you might never know who they really are. Using multiple personas, the ability to post anonymously and lurk (monitor a chat without declaring their presence), and other techniques, predators move around online with no clear identity. A 54-year-old man might tell your daughter he is a 16-year-old high school football star. A con man might pose as your banker trying to verify an electronic payment by asking you to enter the payment amount and your account number.

When you or your child develops a close relationship that exists purely online, consider that you actually have no idea who that other person is or what he or she wants from you. The person might be everything he says he is, or he might be someone entirely different. Often they are a blend of truth and deception. If your child forms many purely online relationships, and spends less time with kids his or her own age offline, consider it a warning.

It is at the moment of conferring trust, of deciding to take the next step in an online relationship, that you put yourself at risk. Children and adults need to recognize the potential risks involved when making the decision to provide more personal information or making a direct connection such as through e-mail, the telephone, and especially meeting in person. The Child Exploitation and Online Protection Centre (CEOP) in the United

Kingdom has said that one in twelve children meets with someone they first encountered online. Comparable research in the United States shows that 12 to 14 percent of teens admit to meeting with Internet friends. What makes this so concerning is that while most people you or your child might go to meet won't be predators, research indicates that more than 90 percent of kids who meet an online predator in person end up being abused (Wolak et al., 2004).

Think About It

You hear a great deal in the news about sexual predators finding victims online, and people often ask me if the number of sexual predators has exploded. In looking at available data, that doesn't seem to be the case. There is a relatively small segment of the population interested in sexually exploiting children. However, some evidence suggests that within this segment there is a growing number of individuals willing to act upon their interests online because of the perceived reduced risks of being caught (Lanning, 2001).

Once you move from the anonymity of a chat room, public social networking site, or discussion board where those you interact with know you only by a nickname, you are potentially entering an unsafe situation. If you post a profile that includes personally, or indirectly, identifiable information that is available *publicly* (to anyone besides your close friends or family), or if you provide contact information such as an e-mail or IM address or a phone number, you have created a situation that allows total strangers to begin using that information in any way they choose to, including breaking through your anonymity while maintaining their own.

What Can You Do?

When you go on a business trip, you or the businesses you come into contact with might routinely take precautions to protect your identity and possessions. Hotels no longer put room numbers on room keys; when you pay at a restaurant using a credit card, you make sure to take your copy of the receipt with you; the message on your home answering machine might say you're not available, but you've learned never to announce that you're out of town for two weeks.

If you use this same logic on the Internet, you can see that there are simple ways to protect your online anonymity and help keep you safer as you move around the Web. The two essential elements to protecting yourself online are to consider *what you are sharing* and *with whom you are sharing it.* To do that

- Make conscious choices about what information you choose to post.

- Make conscious choices about who you share your information with (see Figure 2-1). Don't automatically assume that people you meet online are telling you the truth about their identities or motivations.

Think About It

61 percent of child bloggers, according to David Huffaker's 2004 Georgetown University research project, provide contact information (see Figure 2-2 on the next page).

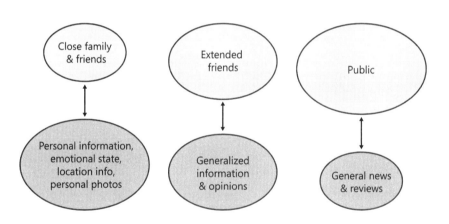

Figure 2-1 The more people you share with, the less personal information you should share.

Distribution of Disclosed Personal Information in Blogs

Figure 2-2 What kids make public in blogs

More specifically, here are some rules of thumb for managing your online anonymity and reducing the risk of becoming a victim.

- Think very, very carefully before providing any direct method of contact to someone you have met only online. You might want to set up a separate e-mail account if you do choose to provide contact information. (See Chapter 10, "Step 7: Understand Risks of Fraudulent Communications and Protect Yourself," for more about how to do this.) Keep in mind that if you provide access to your IM, anybody might be able to see all of your **buddies** as well. Limit your exposure and that of your friends to what you feel is safe.

- Choose nicknames, e-mail addresses, URLs, and other online identifiers that do not reveal your identity (name, gender, age, location) and are not sexually suggestive.

- Be careful when posting visual clues online in photos or videos. (See Chapter 4 for more about revealing visual clues.)

- Be aware that protections you might have put in place on your computer are not protecting you or your child when using a mobile device.

- If you create a profile in a social networking setting, be careful what you include in that profile and to whom you give access.

- If you are using a cell phone that uses location tools such as GPS (global positioning software) and services that share this information with others, be sure you think about who you allow to see this information and when they are allowed to see it.

- Even though being "anonymous" might feel liberating, think twice before you tell total strangers intimate, personal feelings or information that could come back to haunt you.

Think About It

Consider carefully who you count as a friend when providing access to information. Sexual predators are often not strangers. In fact, many of the cases where offenders lured youth online involved family members or acquaintances who used the Internet as a way to supplement their ordinary access to a child. Online they can begin grooming that person in a way that isn't visible to others offline, where the behavior could be seen and cause concern.

- Be careful about providing information that could put somebody else at risk, such as your friends or family. Deliberately putting others at risk for harassment is not only wrong, it might be criminal.

- Services requiring users to sign in and authenticate themselves, such as a members-only Web site, might seem inconvenient, but they are a safeguard for you because they make predators more vulnerable to being identified as they begin to leave an identity trail.

Find Out More

For more advice about how to keep online strangers from finding out your location, see Chapter 7, "Step 4: Don't Let Them Know Where You Live."

CHAPTER THREE

Thinking Like the Enemy: Predatory Behavior

Who are these online predators, and what motivates them to do what they do? The reality might surprise you. An online predator is anyone who preys on others by using the Internet. Like predators in the animal world, they circle the Internet user base looking for easy targets. Easy targets are often the young or old, or those who show weakness.

Usually you encounter criminals only through the media or in courtrooms, but there are criminals and predators in every community and society, and they leverage whatever tools will help them succeed. Cybercriminals prey on the weak just like the garden-variety offline criminals; they're simply using new tools to find opportunities for exploitation.

Just as the Internet is the newest tool in the predator's arsenal, it is also the newest tool in your arsenal. But because you don't make a living using these tools to defend yourself, you are probably still somewhat unfamiliar with the potential risks and how to mitigate them. As a result, you could be more likely to leave openings for cybercriminals—even more so than with the offline predators you've learned to defend against.

In this chapter, I attempt to dispel some misconceptions about who the enemy is, and how he or she thinks, so you can better avoid and defeat predators.

Knowing the Enemy

People online who might do you harm are diverse. They include opportunists who ordinarily are honest but give in to temptation when an opportunity presents itself; people who are angry and want to lash out and harass or hurt an ex-spouse or partner; and segments of the population who have chosen crime as a lifestyle. Officials in countries around the world have been overwhelmed by alarming exposés in the press that named some of the supposedly upstanding citizens caught in child predator "stings": lawyers, doctors, counselors, and employees of law enforcement agencies. But remember, this isn't an Internet-generated phenomenon: It reflects the sad reality that people from all walks of life exploit others for a variety of reasons.

The stereotypes of "creepy guys" and so-called *stranger danger* don't prove to be any truer in the online world than in the offline world. Simply warning those of any age against contact with strangers online or offline misses the point because it doesn't detail the actions or situations you should be watchful for, and it certainly doesn't encompass who you might need to guard against. Table 3-1 is taken from an article in *The Journal of Adolescent Health* by Janis Wolak, JD, David Finkelhor, PhD, and Kimberly Mitchell, PhD, and tells something about who offenders and victims typically are.

Think About It

As Kenneth V. Lanning, former Supervisory Special Agent and profiler with the FBI, has said, "By no reasonable definition can an individual with whom a child has regularly communicated online for months be called a stranger.... In the world of the Internet someone you never met in person is not only not a stranger, but can be your 'best friend.'"

Some predators are indiscriminate—what you could call *equal opportunity offenders* who exploit any weakness in anyone they come across online or offline. Others are more specialized and repeat the same type of crime and/or target the same population segment both online and offline, running cons on the elderly, engineering home break-ins or auto thefts, stealing people's identities, or molesting children.

These people span a range from individuals to loose criminal rings or more formal gangs to organized crime syndicates. They come in all ages, from teens preying on other (often younger) teens to older males and females. Because the Internet has no formal borders, criminals can live in, and strike from, any region of the world.

Table 3-1 A Sampling of the Characteristics of Victims and Dynamics of Internet-Initiated Sex Crimes

Victim's Age	Percent
12	1%
13	26%
14	22%
15	28%
16	14%
17	8%
Victim's Gender	**Percent**
Female	75%
Male	25%
Offender's Age	**Percent**
Under 18	1%
18 to 25	23%
26 to 39	41%
40 or older	35%
Offender's Time of Online Contact Before Meeting Victim	**Percent**
1 month or less	27%
1 to 6 months	48%
More than 6 months	16%
Offender's Type of Online Contact with Victim	**Percent**
Talked to victim by telephone	79%
Sent pictures to victim	48%
Gave or offered victim money or gifts	47%
Sent mail to victim	19%
Communicated with victim online multiple ways	77%

Source: Journal of Adolescent Health, *Vol. 35, No. 5, Wolak et al., 2004*

While some sexual predators simply leverage any opportunity, many look for a victim to whom they feel attracted. Some predators lose interest after children reach a certain age, preferring those under 14 or no older than 7, for example. Typically these people look for vulnerability in the victim: the child, teen, or even adult who projects strong self-esteem is less frequently targeted. Predators might look for a photo that speaks of a shy, self-conscious child, or postings on a blog that express confusion, rebellion, or lack of self-esteem. They are expert at spotting those who have been emotionally or physically neglected.

Some who live on the fringes of the online underworld might or might not commit an actual crime. They might be middlemen who compile your publicly available information into virtual catalogs that they then resell to other criminals who commit the actual crimes (see Figure 3-1).

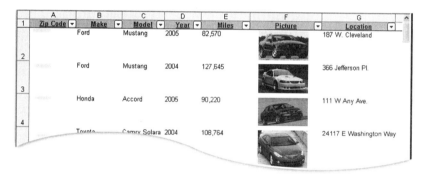

Figure 3-1 A catalog of publicly available information for sale

Anybody who creates, distributes, markets, or views illegal material online can be party to a criminal charge. When you are researching a service or ISP, look for a company that actively protects users from illegal content.

In June 2006, several online industry leaders in the United States joined with the National Center for Missing & Exploited Children (NCMEC) to launch an aggressive new campaign that will develop and deploy technology solutions that disrupt the ability of predators to use the Internet to exploit children or traffic in child pornography.

Think About It

There are not necessarily more dangers in the online world. However, because nobody has taught you how to act safely online, the dangers there seem more intimidating. Comparing and leveraging the safety features provided by different services can help you navigate online and might help inform which services and service providers are right for you.

Recognizing Sexual Predators, Offline and On

As mentioned earlier in this book, sexual predators can "look" like anyone. They can be strangers or people who know you; they might approach your children on their way home from school or while playing in the neighborhood, or befriend them online. Some predators who already know your children use the Internet as a way to make additional contact with them so they can build a "special" bond without you realizing just how much interaction they're having.

Just as you keep an eye on who interacts with your children offline, it's important to have a clear sense of who is contacting your children online, and to be mindful of any changes in their behavior and how they respond to the adults with whom they have contact.

Recognizing predators and predatory behaviors can be complicated, but a great deal of research has been conducted on this topic, and there are many good resources available that can help you. Here are some Web sites to start with: *http://beachildshero.com/traits.htm* and *www.kimberlyscottage. org/obsessed.html*. A good book to reference is *Protecting Your Children From Sexual Predators* by Leigh Baker. You can find additional resources in the back of this book.

You should have an understanding of predatory behaviors, and you should use technology to help you monitor and manage who has access to your children online, and how frequently they are conversing. You can find more information about available tools in "Technology Toolkit" in Part Four of this book. These tools cannot replace your vigilance, but they can go a long way toward providing a safer environment.

How Predators Choose Their Victims

Criminals choose victims for a variety of reasons, but there are some patterns you can identify. Finding a victim to target for an online-initiated crime has three basic steps:

1. Identifying a viable target, whether that target is property or a person.

   If the target is a physical object (a car or house), the predator needs some way to locate the object. Opportunity for access is key—the ability to gain online access to children, young people, or adults as well as any content that helps identify a location for potential offline access is the first goal.

Think About It

Many child sexual predators already knew their victims and used the Internet as a means of facilitating crimes; 50 percent of victims live within a 50-mile radius of their predators (Wolak et al., 2004).

   If the target is a person—child or adult—with whom the predator wants to make physical contact (not just steal their identity), the goal is most often to build a relationship with the victim. The predator starts to collect information that will build an outline of the target and begin to identify them—where they live, what they look like, their name and age, and, to help them make a personal connection, their *emotional state*.

2. Matching the target with what the predator wants.

   If the goal is to get money or tangible goods, such as IDs, cars, or other possessions, the predator sifts through the target's information to find relevant secondary information—photos of a new boat or car, postings where the victim brags about an Xbox or flat-screen TV, references to expensive artwork or jewelry, and so on.

   If physical harm is the predator's objective, then gaining the target's confidence becomes important. The predator wants any information that can help him or her to learn a victim's habits, likes and dislikes, location, and so on.

3. Planning the best time to "strike" and the best method to employ.

    For a burglar this might mean waiting until the target is on vacation. Did you leave a notice on your e-mail to tell people you will be away and will respond next week when you're back, or talk about your upcoming trip on your blog? All of these pieces of information *tell* something about you, and often something about your possessions.

Find Out More

For more information about dealing with those who are out to steal your money or possessions and how to protect yourself, see Chapter 14, "Step 11: Get Savvy About Financial Scams and Fraud."

The Victim Grooming Process

The essential tool a predator uses in **grooming** a victim is one of building up trust. The victim wants somebody to listen to him or her, to understand any self-doubts, to reassure them that they are beautiful, smart, or capable of being popular. To further ingratiate themselves, predators learn their victim's habits, likes, and dislikes and gain their confidence by pretending to share them.

The grooming process also frequently involves giving gifts. By sending gifts to the victim, a predator flatters and makes the victim feel special and somehow indebted.

Think About It

Like offline predators, most individuals attempting to exploit children through the Internet tend to gradually seduce their targets through the use of attention, affection, and gifts.

Another important part of the grooming process is for the predator to drive a wedge between the victim and others in his or her life. If a child, for example, feels his parents don't understand him, or won't let him do things he wants to do, the predator might not only provide that understanding and encouragement, but also enhance the child's sense of unfairness from his parents. This builds a psychological distance from the parents and a psychological dependency on the abuser, which in turn makes it easier for the abuser to continue to groom and/or abuse the child as the child's dependency on approval and support from the predator supersedes that of others. This then provides one rationale for the victim to keep the online relationship secret, and tolerate abuse rather than reach out to those who might protect them.

Who Is Not at Fault

In looking at sexual crimes in particular, one final and very important point to make about these online-initiated crimes is that, like all sexual crimes, there is only one person at fault, and that's the predator.

Chatting with a friend about this book, I talked about how children and teens are unknowingly putting themselves in the path of danger by posting information that allows predators to identify them. His comment, with his 14-year-old son sitting right there, was, "How could they be that stupid? People who put themselves at risk like that have only themselves to blame." He then turned to his son and asked, "Don't they teach you about this at school?"

This is an intelligent, educated man who is a good, conscientious parent. Yet unintentionally he had made two common mistakes. First, he assumed that somebody else is teaching his son the right way to behave online. Second, he made his son feel he is to blame and, in fact, stupid, if he posts information somebody else uses to target him or his family. After these comments, how likely is it that his son would come to him if a problem occurred online as a result of his actions?

Remember, there is only one person at fault when this kind of crime occurs, and it is not the victim. Sexual acts with minors are illegal and exploitive, and as a society, everyone must be committed to protecting minors, even when they act against their own best interests. Taking out your shock on your child if a crime is committed is quite simply wrong, and further alienates your child from you. It is important that the first response they get from you is support and help. Yes, they might have done things that placed them at greater risk, but they are the victim, not the abuser.

It is also important to understand that sexual predators frequently try to make a child believe that the abuse was the child's "fault" or something they "wanted" because if the child feels guilty or ashamed they will be much less likely to report it. Predators make claims such as, "You wouldn't have contacted me if you didn't want it," or "I only did this because I thought it was what you wanted." When a caregiver or authority figure says to an abused child or teen something like "What were you thinking?" or "What was your part in this?" they can be seen as siding with the predator. The parent reinforces that message of guilt and removes the last shreds of hope from the child that they will be believed, nurtured, and protected by those they need support from the most.

A Special Note About Sensitivity to Victims of Sexual Abuse

The following is a quote by Lucy Berliner, Director, Harborview Center for Sexual Assault and Traumatic Stress, and Clinical Associate Professor, University of Washington School of Social Work and Department of Psychiatry and Behavioral Sciences: "Internet sexual exploitation situations often involve a complication in responding to the victims. Although the adult offender is always fully responsible for breaking the law and for taking advantage of the victim, in many cases the victims do not believe they were victimized. They see themselves as involved in a consensual relationship and may not want to cooperate with prosecution or seek treatment for the effects of their victimization experience. It requires great care and skill to connect with the youth and help them come to see the reality of their experience."

It could take many years for the child or teen to realize there was abuse going on. If, in this vulnerable state, it sounds to your child as if you are critical of her actions or blaming her for what happened, she might feel like you are siding with the predator—that it *was* her fault. As a result, you might shatter your child's last hopes for help and support.

As Kenneth Lanning, a special agent with the FBI for more than 30 years, has said in his book titled *Child Molesters: A Behavioral Analysis*, "Child victims can be boys as well as girls, and older as well as younger. Not all child victims are 'little angels.' They are, however, human beings."

As Lanning points out, it's important to remember that your child is a victim even when he or she has used poor judgment or made mistakes. As a society, people sometimes struggle to identify who the victim is in an abuse case. It might be hard to accept, for example, that a prostitute can be a victim, even if she initiated contact. No matter what a young child or teen has initiated, children are *always* the victims if they are abused mentally or physically by an adult.

Blaming the victim might in fact drive them into the arms of other online "friends" for comfort, and will certainly minimize the likelihood that they'll tell you about other instances or issues. You need to be very careful to work with any victim to help them heal from the experience and become more educated about risks.

Find Out More

What can you do if you find that someone you know is a victim of an online crime? See Chapter 18, "It Takes Everyone to Make a Safe Internet," for specific steps you can take.

The chapters in the next part of this book provide further insight into predator behavior, and specific steps you can take to remain as safe online as you do in your own home or town.

PART TWO

13 Steps to Internet Security

CHAPTER FOUR

Step 1: Be Careful What You Show People

Brittany runs up the front steps and dashes in the front door of her house one afternoon, excited because her mom was going to make a trip to the electronics superstore that day to buy a new digital camera. They've been talking about getting a better one for ages, but they finally saw this model on sale with all the cool features her mom and dad liked and they decided to buy it.

While her mom studies the manual, Brittany puts on her favorite sweater and jeans. Her mom takes a picture of Brittany posing in front of their house leaning on their car.

She's always been a little shy about having her picture taken, but because she's wanted to post some photos on her new blog, she's a little excited, too. She set up her blog to make it available to anybody so she could meet lots of new people. All her new online "friends" will now be able to see her house and what she looks like. Brittany also snapped a photo of the store across the street because she had talked about it in a recent blog entry.

With the camera in hand, Brittany heads upstairs to the spare bedroom where they keep the computer, opens up her blog, and uploads the pictures from the new camera. She adds a few comments, and then logs off.

Later that evening, a man sits at his computer a few towns away. Within a few minutes of opening Brittany's blog, he knows the town she lives in, her street address, and phone number. He also knows her age and interests–plenty of information to aid him in locating and grooming his next victim.

What Just Happened?

If a picture paints a thousand words, just what are our pictures saying to online predators? Neither Brittany nor her mother realized it, but the two photos that Brittany posted, shown in Figures 4-1 and 4-2, give important clues to a would-be predator. Can you spot them?

Figure 4-1 Brittany, with her house and family car

This photo shows their house number, helping a predator to pinpoint her location (especially easy to do because Brittany has included her city and state in her blog profile). Brittany is giving away not only an image of herself that can be used to identify her if a predator goes to her home, school, or one of her favorite hangouts, but she is also giving an idea of her approximate age and socioeconomic status. The photo also shows the family car with the license plate in full view.

In Figure 4-2, the street signs in the view from her house identify the cross streets where Brittany's house is located. And the store across the street displays its name in large letters. Anybody could go online and locate that store, find out the town and state where it's located, get a map of that town, and know exactly where Brittany lives.

Figure 4-2 The view from Brittany's house

Find Out More

In Chapter 7, "Step 4: Don't Let Them Know Where You Live," I go into more detail about the risks of revealing your location through the information you post online and the devices and services you use.

Think About It

It takes me an average of nine minutes to get the following information about a potential victim from the typical blog: full name and address; a map showing the location of their home and school (using some online 3-D mapping services, you can even get a satellite photo of a person's home just by typing in their address); phone number; photos to identify the person; names of their close friends and family members; their school; their clubs, hobbies, and interests; and their emotional state. For girls, I can often add height and weight to the list.

Assessing the Risks

People can send visual images such as photos and videos out into the world in a variety of ways. Images can be sent via e-mail or instant messaging, uploaded to blogs, and posted in online auctions, in classified ads, or on discussion boards. Sending images that identify you or your location isn't the problem. Posting them publicly is. Putting images where anyone can view them can create risk if you have not been taught how to look at these images through a predator's eyes, and become conscious about exactly what information you are sharing.

Think About It

According to Consumer Reports WebWatch, half of Internet users (47 percent) say that, while browsing, they have seen digital images that have been manipulated. Tens of thousands of images have been manipulated in some way for a wide variety of reasons. Some people touch up images to make them clearer or to be funny; some are committing fraud; and still others are out to make money from the billion-dollar pornography industry.

What Forms of Visual Information Put You at Risk?

The potential risks in posting identifying images publicly don't stop with photos uploaded from your computer. Two other forms of images pose a risk: videos and **videocam** feeds. These images might be made public through a computer, mobile phone, game console, or other devices.

Video and **Voice over IP (VoIP)** technologies are a great way for grandparents, friends, and even parents who travel to stay in touch with their kids. These technologies remove the barrier of typing that young children and some elderly people struggle with. They allow for a natural flow of conversation.

But the flip side of this particular coin is that video and VoIP also allow predators to communicate with those very young children who can't type, widening their field of potential victims. These audio and visual messages also can't be tracked by parental control software yet, as some text-based communications can be.

Video cameras (also called videocams or webcams) make it possible to send a live image of yourself out onto the Web. It's in the nature of many predators to want to see as much of their victims as they can. They encourage victims to show more of themselves or their surroundings in videocam images. A child can progress from taking his shirt off when sitting by the pool at the urging of a predator to providing live sex shows for money. Each small step in between will seem innocent, only a small increment in the process, until the child is hooked on the money and/or attention he or she begins to crave.

A predator uses such images for a variety of purposes, from simply viewing them for a thrill to selling them or using them to blackmail the victim into further cooperation. These images can even be used to train new victims about behaviors the predator wants them to emulate.

Not every videocam show is homegrown. Technology advances actually allow scheduled sex-abuse broadcasts, often involving children. These occur live for potentially large audiences who can participate virtually from around the world. People actually subscribe to these shows, just as you subscribe to a cable channel. Catalogs of potential victims are available to allow the viewing audience to pick the program and even to select new targets that match their interests.

Find Out More

Check out a revealing article about a real-life webcam sex scandal in the December 19, 2005 *New York Times:* "Through His Webcam, a Boy Joins a Sordid Online World" (*www.nytimes.com/2005/12/19/national/19kids.ready.html?ei=5090&en=aea51b391 9b2361a&ex=1292648400&partner=rssuserland&emc=rss&pagewanted=print*). The teenage boy discussed in this article eventually became a videocam porn star, lured by the money a predator offered him, as well as the attention he received.

Protecting Yourself

I don't advocate that you never post a picture or make use of a webcam. There are far too many positive uses of image and video sharing. What I do suggest is that, when you are in a forum where what you post is available to the public, you take the time to make sure you aren't broadcasting visual information that can put you or your family at risk. Here's what you can do to help protect yourself.

Make sure you study any image you post, e-mail, instant message, or send through your cell phone for the following types of clues to your identity and location:

- Street address via a house number or street signs

- Car model or car license plate

- Your unaltered physical appearance that can be used to identify you (Your eye, your shoes, or your hand would be safe; a complete image of your face wouldn't.)

- Where you work or attend school

- Places you go on a regular basis (Showing yourself in the mall is fine, but showing yourself outside the Springfield Mall on Route 3 isn't!)

Here are some additional steps you can take to limit your risk when posting visual images online that you make available to the public:

- Use an image-editing program to slightly alter images of yourself; for example, you might blur your eyes or place a black rectangle over them, to "hide" your visual identity from predators, as shown in Figure 4-3.

Think About It

Remember, if you post a picture of yourself or your children post their pictures, anybody in the world can also manipulate those images, placing the head of one person on a different body, for example. Altering any picture you share with the public to be unidentifiable can save you from this form of exploitation and embarrassment.

- Keep your webcam hooked up to a computer that you keep in a public place in your home, not behind closed doors. However, be aware that webcams are relatively inexpensive and your child could buy one and set it up when you're not at home. Talk to your children about the dangers of posting any image of themselves that's available to the general public online.

- Check to see if your child's mobile phone has video capabilities.

- Talk to your children about how predators might exploit them using visual images. Make sure they understand that it is illegal to possess or participate in creating child pornography.

- Help your children recognize when requests for images by strangers could be unusual and dangerous.

- Discuss the long-term consequences of how a video with sexual overtones might be used later against you or your child: It might be resold, posted online, sent to your school or place of work, or used as evidence in a trial. Such an image might even show up years later to hurt your child when he or she applies for college or a job or becomes a parent.

House number

Appearance

License plate

Cross streets

Landmark

Figure 4-3 Brittany's photos, with the street address and her appearance protected

CHAPTER FIVE

Step 2: Don't Tell People More Than You Should

Kathy came from an upper middle-class family near Toronto. She had a master's degree in finance and a rewarding job as the assistant manager of a local bank. She enjoyed reading and movies, and played tennis with her friends every weekend.

Sadly, Kathy's husband Roger had died five years before of cancer. Her nine-year-old daughter, Carrie, had been the joy of their lives, coming as she did in Kathy's late 30s. In fact, it was Carrie who suggested that her mom try blogging as a way to help her work through her grief after Roger's death.

Kathy found that she enjoyed the social networking activity of blogging. She had set up her blog to be available to the public and had organized it around three main themes: her husband's death, how she was dealing with her grief, and her personal likes and interests. She found that many people had similar interests and personal experiences and sympathized with her.

How could this therapeutic outlet put her at risk? Suppose one day Kathy notices that entries from a man named William are especially appealing to her. He seems to like the same books and movies, and because his wife died a few years earlier, he understands her loneliness and how hard it is to lose a spouse. Eventually she might give William her e-mail address. She might find she looks forward to receiving his messages.

This could be the start to a wonderful new relationship, or William could be a con man who preys on the loneliness and vulnerability of widows. One day she might get an e-mail from William saying that he wants to meet her in person. Kathy might unknowingly agree to meet a complete stranger who is targeting her because of what she revealed about herself online.

What Just Happened?

I came across Kathy's blog, shown in Figure 5-1, one afternoon, by performing a search with three common keywords: blog, vacation, and teenager.

On browsing through her blog, I found that Kathy, a 47-year-old seasoned blogger who'd had a site for over three years, was articulate and well read. Yet, she had unknowingly provided all the information necessary to

- Run an online phone book search and find her full address and phone number

- Obtain a satellite photo of her home using free online mapping tools

- Learn her e-mail address (she posts it in her blog)

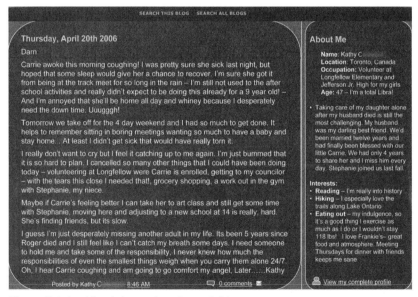

Figure 5-1 Leaking information through blogs

- Know from her writing that she is lonely and grieving over her dead spouse and that she's missing adult company

- Learn that she has a nine-year-old daughter and a niece living in her home

- Learn her hobbies and interests, favorite movies and books, and even her weight loss history (she's down to 118 pounds)

It took me four minutes to get information about Kathy, including her address, phone number, workplace, personal history, emotional state, family situation, and weight.

With the information she's provided, Kathy has opened herself up to having her identity stolen, her house broken into, or even potentially being physically abused. A man studying her interests and background could transform himself into her "dream" man by sharing her likes and use that advantage in a variety of ways. He could also use that connection to get to her daughter or niece.

When I contacted Kathy, I started by asking her if she felt she understood the risks of posting information online. She said she did. When I expressed concern over what her blog contents revealed about her, she reacted with disbelief that anybody could locate her through information in her blog.

"How do you think I got your phone number?" I asked. There was a silence on the other end of the phone line. Suddenly Kathy seemed to take my call more seriously.

When she realized the danger she had placed herself and her daughter and niece in, Kathy's reaction was one of anger that her blog host had not advised her about the risks of posting personal information online to the public. Unfortunately, this is all too common. Most blog/social networking companies default users to a "Public" profile, which gives them the best revenue opportunity. It is then up to the user to figure out how to change the settings if they want to limit the number of people they share their space with.

Keep in mind that publicly viewable blogs are great for sharing publicly appropriate information. The trouble begins when you place *private* information on a publicly viewable site, whether a blog, discussion board, or chat room.

What Is Social Networking?

In the world of computers, networking refers to two computers communicating with each other. Social networking is a term that refers to people communicating with people. Online this occurs in settings that include blogs, chat rooms, discussion boards, instant messaging, and e-mail. Your *trusted network* is made up of people you know, or whom you trust (for example, the friend of a friend). A *casual network* is made up of people you don't know and don't yet trust. Unfortunately, in online social networking settings, people often blur the distinction between those they trust and those they shouldn't because they lack physical clues about people and make assumptions about their anonymity online. It's also important to note that one social networking forum—blogs—can be set up to be either available to the public (the casual network) or kept private (limited to the trusted network).

Assessing the Risks

Just as there are risks from posting visual images (see Chapter 4, "Step 1: Be Careful What You Show People"), there are risks in posting text online. One important thing to understand is that it's not merely a single piece of information that typically does the damage. It's the accumulation of information out there about you that seals the deal for predators. That information might not even come from a single source. Predators might learn your first name from your instant messaging identity, your state from your blog profile, the college you went to from a blog entry, your current occupation from your school Web site's alumni section, your phone number from a white pages search, and so on. Before long, they have gathered enough information to come knocking on your front door or assume your identity.

Think About It

A common way to let others know you'll be out of town is to set up an away message in your e-mail program (see Figure 5-2). An away message automatically sends a reply to any messages that arrive, telling the senders you'll be away from your office or home. You should be careful about letting just anybody who e-mails you know your whereabouts. If a predator has figured out where you live, announcing that you're out of town for a defined period of time is practically an invitation to rob you.

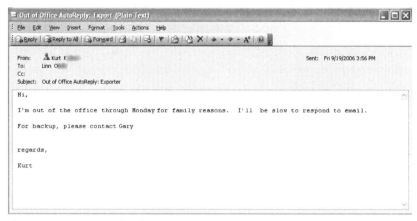

Figure 5-2 An example of an away message

Remember that 50 percent of bloggers say they blog as a form of emotional therapy. Sharing information about your emotional state might seem harmless if you believe you are anonymous online. (See Chapter 2, "Misperceptions About Online Anonymity," for more about this.) Because you are often less anonymous than you believe, advertising your vulnerabilities beyond your closest circle of friends is seldom a good idea.

Protecting Yourself

I recommended to Kathy that if she wanted to have a publicly viewable blog, she should remove her last name, her location information, any mention of her place of employment, and the name of her deceased husband. She should also avoid displaying her emotional vulnerability in her writing. The other option would be to share any information she wants to, but that she restrict access to the blog to her friends and family.

> ### Think About It
> Do you like to let others know about your newest purchase, fancy house, or upcoming expensive vacation? Talking about your possessions in a public forum is like waving a red flag in front of a predator: It draws attention to hot items they might steal, and provides information on how to flatter your taste or accomplishments.

Pay attention to whom you share information with. Sharing information with close friends and family poses little risk; sharing with online "friends" you have never met is riskier. As the circle of people you share with widens, so does your risk. An example of this type of danger is the older person who posts family tree information on a publicly accessible genealogy site. When that long-lost cousin calls, is it any surprise he wants to borrow money? Also, if the blogger has included her mother's maiden name on the genealogy site, she might be handing over everything a cyber-criminal needs to steal her identity.

Be aware of whether you are posting information about others that could endanger them, or if they are posting information about you. For example, if you mention your friend's blog on your own site, a predator might go there and read an entry that mentions that you just broke up with your boyfriend and are depressed. That entry might provide your last name. Unwittingly, your friend has just provided the predator with a tool he can use to connect with you and gain your trust.

Think About It

The William W. Maddux Kellogg School of Management performed a study that showed people have a natural tendency to trust those they have any connection with. If a predator has your name and your friend's name, you've given him a way to use you to build a connection to your friend.

Remember, if you don't make information publicly available, you significantly reduce potential risks. If you go the public route, simply be thoughtful about what you say. This doesn't take a lot of time or effort. Read through what you've written before you post it and consider, just for a minute, if anything you've said identifies you or gives away information about you or others that would be useful to someone with bad intentions.

Just as it's become second nature for you to avoid providing certain personal information in a conversation with a stranger, it will quickly become second nature for you to protect yourself in online interactions.

CHAPTER SIX

Step 3: Be Alert to How Predators Prey on Emotions

Steve H. usually liked his job as public defender in a small suburban town just outside of Dallas, but today he dreaded the task ahead. He was scheduled to meet with a new client, Randall M. Randall was a sex offender who had been caught stalking children online. With an 8-year-old boy and a 13-year-old girl at home, Steve found the thought of interviewing Randall about his alleged crimes to be upsetting.

The jailer settled Steve into the visitor's conference room, and a moment later led Randall through the door. Dressed in a green cotton jumpsuit, Randall was clean-shaven but looked every bit of his 51 years. Steve jumped right into the questioning and found Randall wasn't the least bit reluctant to talk about his "interests," as he called them. In fact, he seemed to enjoy talking about what he did and took pride in his talent at grooming victims.

"This kid, Kit? I zeroed in on him as a victim real fast. He's 14 and lives in a small town. Small-town kids feel isolated and crave outside contact. After all, they've met everybody in town. They're also a little less sophisticated than the city kids and more trusting of people, so it's easier to get one over them. Small-town kids are also a good bet to take you up on an invite to come to the big city for the day to meet.

"It was a cinch to get his address and phone number, so I called him a few times. He didn't even question how I got his phone number—just seemed flattered that some big-city kid felt like spending time with him. He'd said

online he hated to see people sad, so I hooked into that. I told him my friend had died in a car accident. He seemed to want to comfort me, which is a great way to build a connection."

Steve shifted uncomfortably in his chair, repelled by the "tricks of the trade" this online stalker was sharing. This man who preyed on children was actually smug. Steve fought back the urge to get up and leave. He had to defend this guy, but he didn't have to like it.

"His messages kept mentioning how he'd fight with his parents. His dad was a real cold fish, and you could tell the kid craved affection. I gave him attention, gifts, a lot of praise, you know. Sent him some dirty magazines and told him not to tell his folks about me 'cause they wouldn't like him getting that kind of stuff. He ate it up. Kids that age, they just aren't that great at figuring out what motivates other people, you know?"

*Steve thought of his own kids and wondered if they would trust him enough to tell him if this type of thing was happening to them. Randall shifted in his seat and started talking again, as if reading Steve's mind. "Not that their parents are usually any better—I usually spend as much time manipulating the kid's parents as I spend grooming the kid, so they trust me being around him." Randall chuckled to himself and shook his head in wonder. "And it's dead easy. Most people are so gullible, I swear they **want** to be victims."*

During the drive home that afternoon, Steve's hands were shaking as he thought about his own children—about what emotional buttons someone like Randall could push with them. As he pulled into his driveway, he knew the first thing he had to do was hold them both close. Then he would sit down and have a good, long talk with them.

What Just Happened?

Randall is typical of online predators who become expert at gauging who will make a good victim. He knows that adolescents in particular have a need to form new relationships, and that kids from rural areas who have limited access to new people are frequently more open to online relationships. Kit's blog, shown in Figure 6-1, provides several clues to Kit's emotional state, such as an entry about a fight with his parents and another where he states that he can't wait to get out of his small town.

By introducing sex into their conversation and sending gradually more graphic pornography to Kit, Randall was able to manipulate the teen into staying silent about their relationship. What 14-year-old kid would admit to his parents that he's getting pornography from a friend? Eventually most sexual predators convince a child that he or she is a willing participant in the sexual exploitation and that what happens is at least partly their fault. This approach uses the victim's guilt to prevent them from revealing what's going on to others who might intervene.

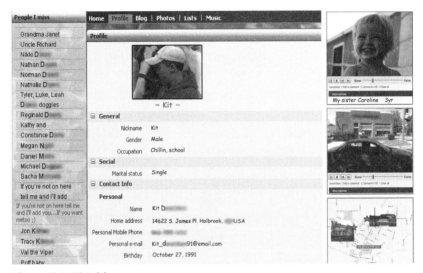

Figure 6-1 Kit's blog

According to law enforcement officers, including Kenneth Lanning, and mental health professionals, predators are so good at building up this trusting relationship that many victims don't feel they are being abused until years later. They come to believe that what's happening is a form of love relationship.

Think About It

How prevalent is the sexual exploitation of minors in general? Every two and a half minutes, somewhere in America, someone is sexually assaulted. About 44 percent of rape victims in the United States are under 18 years of age (*www.rainn.org*).

Assessing the Risks

The exact number of sexual predators online at any given time is unknown, but some estimates go as high as tens of thousands. Some have a snatch-and-grab attack as their goal. But for others who want to perpetrate a scam or create a relationship of extended sexual abuse, they are trying first and foremost to gain their victim's trust.

As Lawrence Likar, a former FBI supervisor, has said about the vulnerability of some victims of sexual abuse, "There are problems in their own lives that make them predisposed to manipulation by adults. The predators know that and are able to tap into these problems and offer what appear to be solutions."

Predators know that forming relationships is a developmental imperative of adolescence to fulfill a need for intimacy, self-validation, and companionship, and they play on that need. They also know that a disproportionate number of teens who are exploited online have difficult home relationships and are looking for support they don't get from their parents.

But it's not just children and teens who are at risk. The predators' tools for manipulation, which allow them to build trust, take advantage of emotional vulnerability, and spot people who don't get the love and support they need in their lives, can be used on anybody, at any age, and for a variety of reasons.

Protecting Yourself

Because cybercriminals exploit weakness and prey on vulnerabilities, it's important that you and your family understand that broadcasting fears and insecurities online to strangers is a bad idea. Just as walking down the street with an assertive, self-confident air will discourage a mugger from picking you out as a victim, projecting a positive attitude online will help you avoid an online predator.

Watch Your Own Behavior

If you make an online "friend" who seems to make it his business to learn your likes, dislikes, and preferences, and then flatters you, think twice about that person's motivations. Gifts and money are inappropriate from somebody you don't know. You should know that, and your kids should, too.

If you are publishing content that you make available to the public, avoid giving clues to your feelings. Text clues to your emotions are phrases such as "I'm sad," "I'm lonely," or "I just had a fight with my parents [or spouse, or boyfriend]." Use of emoticons (see Figure 6-2) that suggest a vulnerable emotional state can increase your potential risk. Even your body language in a photo can show your emotional state.

Figure 6-2 Emoticons add dimension to your online conversations but can also make you vulnerable to manipulation by predators.

Find Out More

See Chapter 18, "It Takes Everyone to Make a Safe Internet," for guidance on creating a family discussion guide that helps you and your family recognize warning signs of predators preying on your kids' emotions.

Of course, the most difficult aspect of the fact that predators exploit your emotions is that those who are emotionally vulnerable don't always show good judgment. If a child feels alienated from his or her parents, or a wife from her husband, for example, the lack of support and affection in their lives is what puts them at risk, and that can't be fixed overnight. Others also at risk include those struggling with depression, anxiety, or loneliness, and especially boys struggling with questions about their own sexuality (Lanning, 2001). But if you and your family are at least informed about the ways that predators play on these vulnerabilities, you might help avoid the emotional and physical abuse that will only add to the emotional burden that already exists.

Think About It

A service that allows users to send gifts or in any other way reward others might expose them to the grooming activity a predator uses to build trust with a potential victim.

Looking for Telltale Signs

Evidence of exploitation or grooming is not always easy to spot. Here are some signs to look for that might indicate children are becoming victims of predatory behavior. However, keep in mind that many of these signs are also fairly typical online teen behavior. These are things you should be aware of and that are worth discussing, but the actions alone aren't proof that predation is occurring:

- Your child spends large amounts of time online, especially at night, and is secretive about whom they are communicating with.

- You find pornography on the computer.

- Your child receives gifts or mail from someone you don't know, or from someone you do know but who you might not expect to pay your child that kind of attention.

- Your child gets phone calls from or places long distance calls to a person you don't know.

- Your child becomes even more withdrawn from the family, possibly also alienating themselves from their friends.

- Your child sets up alternate or additional user accounts.

Getting the Message Across to Your Kids

How do you convince your children to avoid sharing too much information with people they don't know online? Several times, when I've seen blogs where kids have exposed themselves to risk, I've placed this comment: "Imagine the creepiest stranger you can think of. If you ran into this person on a dark street, would you share this kind of information with him? If the answer is no, why are you placing it in *public* on the Internet?" In every case, those teens had made sure their blogs were no longer available *to the public* within hours.

CHAPTER SEVEN

Step 4: Don't Let Them Know Where You Live

A man approached me after one of my lectures on online safety. He was well dressed and exhibited a professional, confident attitude. But there was an undercurrent of unease I commonly see after my online safety presentations as people reflect on their own online postings. They wonder whether they are comfortable with the choices they have made.

Ed told me his 15-year-old son had been blogging for a year or so, and he wanted him to know about the dangers I'd just outlined. But, Ed said with a touch of sadness in his expression, he felt his son, John, wouldn't listen to him. He asked if I'd take a look at John's blog and send him a note about any ways in which he might be putting himself at risk.

I reviewed John's site that evening. Here's a portion of the letter I wrote to John:

"You have a cool blog, and you're young, good-looking, and invincible, right? Maybe not. Let me start by saying your dad didn't give me any information about you other than a link to your space. No tricks involved.

"From your blog, I know your full name, age, school, city, and that you're new to the school and want a girlfriend. How long does it take me to find you at your school or your house just by using the information you provided in your blog? Do these aerial photos look familiar? [See Figures 7-1 and 7-2 on the next page.]

Figure 7-1 John's school

Figure 7-2 John's house

"Your blog shows your folks can afford to send you to private schools, and you mention flat-screen TVs and other expensive stuff in your house. Think about how easy it would be for someone who can already get your address to break in to your home, or pass the info to someone else who is looking for flat-screen TVs to steal.

"Think the only people reading your blog are your friends? Think again."

What Just Happened?

John is typical of many people who are unaware that there are criminals out there compiling virtual catalogs or databases of publicly available information, including people's locations and possessions. Location is a key element in crime because access is key. That access could be to you, your family, your home, or your possessions.

John had left clues that made it easy for me to find his school and home. Even the address of his date for the homecoming dance, whose picture he had posted, was not hard to find. I didn't have to know a thing about him to get this information in just minutes. He had shared information about his school, his family's possessions, his friends, and his habits, such as where he liked to hang out and activities that kept him late at school on certain days. By exposing his location, John was putting not only himself but also his friends and family at risk.

Assessing the Risks

To meet a victim, a predator has to know where to find that person or arrange a place to meet. To rob you, a predator has to know where to find your house. People might provide this information in a variety of ways: inadvertently through photos (see Chapter 4, "Step 1: Be Careful What You Show People," for one example) or through text where they list their full names, the part of the country or the city they live in, their employer or school, and so on.

Why Do They Care Where You Live?

The reality is that 52 percent of teen victims of Internet-initiated sexual abuse travel less than 10 miles to an initial meeting with a predator, and in 50 percent of cases, victims and predators travel a combined total of less than 50 miles to meet (Wolak et al., 2004). From a predatory point of view, it is simply more convenient to find victims in the same general area.

The risk is not just in blogs. Text in any publicly viewable communication might reveal your location (see Figure 7-3 on the next page). For example, in an instant messaging session you can display information about your location via

- Your personal message or profile
- A **buddy search**
- Voice conversations
- A video giving visual clues to your surroundings
- Mapping functionality that shows IM buddies satellite images in which they can locate where you are

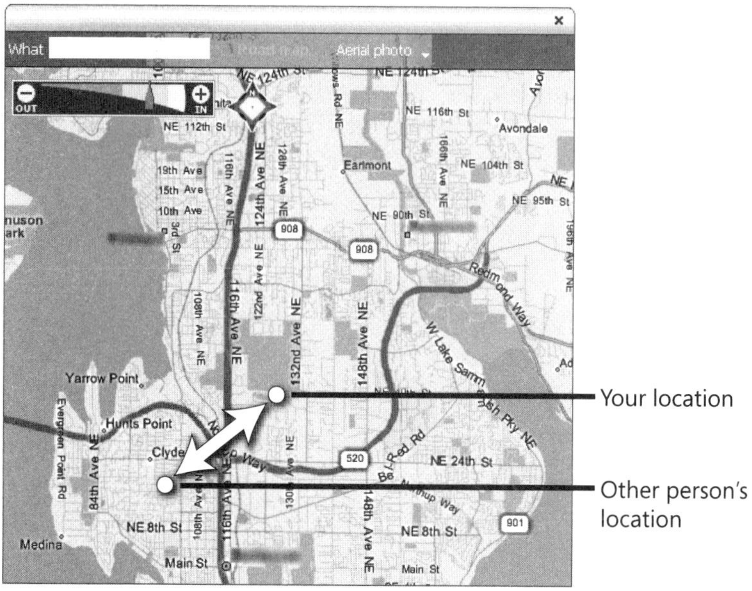

Figure 7-3 Location is a key element in predation.

Filtering applications allow you to block certain sites that have inappropriate content, but if a site does not get flagged by such an application, that's not enough to protect your identity or location. Once you access any site, you can share any information you wish, including your location. It often doesn't occur to young people how someone might use this information, not only about them, but also about their friends and everybody in their entire household.

Think About It

The initial face-to-face meeting of a child with a sexual predator met online takes place in the victim's own home 20 percent of the time. Another 19 percent occur in the predator's home (Wolak et al., 2004).

Location Application Dangers

Applications that allow you to pinpoint a friend's location might seem cool, but consider the safety measures and features a predator could take advantage of:

- There are programs available that allow kids to download a **location application** to their phone that then beacons to their friends, and to friends of friends, with their exact location.

- Other programs take location sharing in a slightly different direction. They send a beacon not only to other mobile devices, but also allow desktop computer users to track you. This feature is being touted, among other things, as a way for parents to keep an eye on their kids. Who else is keeping an eye on them? Is this feature being used to keep an eye on you? Would you know if it were?

- Yet other programs expand the location process by enabling users to chat instantly and view the locations of *all* other members of the chat. No sign-up is required; all you do is begin to type into the chat field. It took 24 seconds the first time I visited a site like this for sex to become a chat topic.

And keep in mind that the danger isn't limited to your desktop computer; most mobile devices these days offer opportunities to find you (see Figure 7-4).

Figure 7-4 Location risks from mobile devices

Technology Makes Finding You Easier

In fact, finding you is becoming much easier with new technologies, and this has both benefits and risks. Cell phones, for example, broadcast location information constantly when the power is on. With over 2 billion wireless users worldwide, tracking a huge number of people without their knowledge has become more of a reality than ever before.

Think About It

According to Informa Telecoms & Media, in many countries, the penetration of wireless technology in the marketplace is at or near 100 percent of the population. Even in the United States, where the number is lower, over 214 million Americans (about two out of three) are cellular subscribers.

Many new cars and trucks are now equipped with location systems that provide maps and emergency services to drivers. Cell phones are being upgraded to ensure that ambulances and law enforcement can find you if you need help. Some transportation departments have begun tracking wireless signals from devices in cars to identify traffic problems. Many companies have begun monitoring their fleet of vehicles and/or shipments of goods to help improve their business models and service levels. Law enforcement and intelligence agencies are gathering invaluable information about criminals and their activities. Parents are monitoring their children's whereabouts.

But there are safety and privacy implications with location features that you should discuss with family and friends. Web services exist that allow users to broadcast their location to all their IM buddies. Services that enable parents to track a child (which you might or might not feel is appropriate, based on circumstances) can also be used to track spouses, girlfriends and boyfriends, and so on. Carefully consider who, if anyone, should be tracking you and your family members, and talk about the implications of using these services with your family.

Your device's location can generally be tracked in one of three ways:

1. Global Positioning System (GPS) uses satellites in space to compare the timing of radio signals and can be accurate to within about 20 yards.

2. Wi-fi networks track millions of radio signals from transmitters in urban areas, though the individual radio signal is anonymous.

3. Triangulation collects information from two or three cell towers to help pinpoint the location of a device.

Protecting Yourself

It might be obvious to you that you shouldn't post your home address on a blog. But did you stop to think that you might be revealing your home address and telephone number or cell phone number in the signature line attached to each out-of-office message automatically sent to anybody and everybody who e-mails you in your absence? Did you remember you were wearing a T-shirt from your company picnic or your teen was wearing a sweatshirt with her high school name on it in that picture you posted on your blog? Could somebody put together your house number on the picture of your home with the city and state you included in your profile in order to find you?

There are times when you might choose to post contact information—for example, when posting a résumé—but first consider who will be able to see that information. Will the posting be available to the general public? Do you need to provide a complete address, or would an e-mail address and state suffice?

As with every other topic in this book, the first goal in protecting your location is awareness of potential pitfalls. Then you can decide if you are comfortable with the information you've shared, and who you've shared it with, or if there are additional steps you want to take to prevent giving away your location. Here are some steps to consider:

- Don't leave yourself vulnerable to a simple phone directory lookup. If you post your full name and city on your site, finding you becomes a much simpler task. Don't post your last name on your site, and don't use other people's full names or anything else that specifically identifies them. Your friends already know this information, and it's nobody else's business.

- Remove any information that helps someone locate your home, school, where you work, and even your town, especially if it's a small town, which makes you easier to find.

- Consider whether you want your blog/social networking site/space to be public or not. The wider the access, the less specific the information you should share.

- Be aware of what you're showing in photos that might identify your location or say more about you than you intend. This includes clothing with logos or names, car license plate, street signs, and anything else in the background that gives clues to where you are. (Remember Brittany from Chapter 4 and the photos she posted of her house, car, and neighborhood.)

- Be savvy about what your friends are sharing about you on their blogs and through comments on your site; it might not be you who is exposing your location.

- Be alert to new technologies offered by your service providers, or that your kids learn about, that might share your location information through cell phones and other mobile devices.

CHAPTER EIGHT

Step 5: Don't Expose Yourself Through Instant Messaging

Jim just started working in the accounting department at an international high-tech company. Coming from a job in the more conservative publishing industry, he was impressed by all the technology people used in their work. The company provided all employees in his division with **smartphones** *or* **PDAs** *for instant messaging, accessing the company's wireless network to read e-mail on the run, and tracking contacts and appointments.*

By the end of his second week, Jim had received many requests from people asking to be on his IM buddy list, so getting two more wasn't surprising. Thinking these were from co-workers, he clicked Accept. When he turned on the phone Saturday morning to show his 10-year-old daughter all the cool stuff it could do, he noticed that his new "buddies" were online. He clicked on the profile of one, and was surprised to be taken to a teen-girl's blog with definite sexual overtones. He quickly went to his settings to block that buddy from future contact. While blocking the first contact, a message appeared from the other one: "Hi, cute guy. Wanna party?"

Embarrassed in front of his daughter, Jim immediately blocked that contact as well and deleted both, explaining sheepishly that he had made a mistake by letting those people on his IM list. Then he went in search of his wife to tell her what had happened—before their daughter did.

What Just Happened?

Instant messaging enables immediate interaction between people. But one of the great features of IM—its real-time interaction—opens a window for unsavory people and information to get through. That's because, unlike e-mail, instant messages and requests to be added to your IM list of buddies come while you are signed on, and usually you respond to them then and there. That often pushes people, like Jim, to make instant decisions about whom they will allow to be a contact. It's so easy to assume that the person requesting to be your buddy is someone you know. Once somebody is accepted onto your list of buddies, that person can potentially see when you are signed on to an IM session and can communicate with you, can send you pictures, videos, or other files, might be able to see everyone on your buddy list and communicate with them, and with some of the new features coming on the market, might even be able to see your exact physical location.

Jim got caught by two spam-like messaging campaigns that count on people to accept their requests, either because they believe they're being contacted by someone they know, or simply because they accept them without thinking about it. This phenomenon of spam being delivered via instant messaging is referred to as "**spim**" (spam + IM = spim) and is growing by leaps and bounds.

What Is Instant Messaging?

Most people think of an instant messaging program as just a way to let people connect and chat in real time using text messages. Once simply a text-based product, IM has in recent years added features that allow you to hold voice conversations, send photos and files, show live videocam feeds of participants, and receive and send e-mail. Some IM services also allow you to search the Web, locate others by using GPS or other location technologies, listen to music, watch videos, customize your experiences with free and **for-pay items** such as winks and avatars, play games, and share applications. It is even possible to give a buddy **remote access** to your computer and computer applications.

You might get a message from someone who claims to have met you the other day. The message often invites you to click on a link to see that person via webcam, or to visit their blog. Because you're embarrassed that you can't remember this person, you might think that viewing a picture of him or her would be a good idea. You click a link, and before you know it you're routed to a pornographic blog or some other inappropriate site. What's worse is that once you're there, clicking the Close button to try to exit the site might bring up similar sites. Shutting them all down could involve rebooting your computer, removing spyware, and resetting your home page.

But then there are all the positive features of IM. IM enables you to stay in touch with friends and family (see Figure 8-1). With IM you can also view other people's profiles and blogs, send text messages to mobile phones, and use mini-programs called **bots** to perform searches or other tasks. IM is available on your computer, through game consoles, and through mobile devices such as cell phones and PDAs.

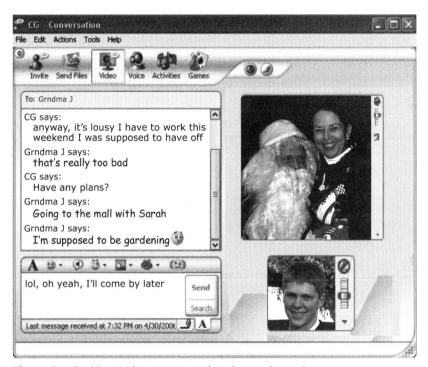

Figure 8-1 Positive IM between grandmother and grandson

Assessing the Risks

If you aren't familiar with all the features offered by IM programs today, you should check them out and understand how to use them so you can make informed choices about what is and isn't appropriate for you and your family. Features such as remote assistance (which gives you the ability to allow somebody in another location to access your computer to help you solve a technical problem, but which can also be used maliciously by someone to whom you have given access to view sensitive files and saved passwords) and video conversations that feed live images between people enable some troubling scenarios for those who don't use them wisely.

> ### Think About It
> According to Georgetown University research results released in April 2004, 44 percent of kids reveal their IM address in their blogs, and most of their blogs are open to the public, allowing anyone to communicate with them or send files, photos, bots, and more.

For teens, who often consider the size of their IM buddy list to be a status symbol, clicking the Accept button to allow people to join their list of contacts is often a given. Unfortunately, not everybody who asks to be your buddy is somebody you would want as a friend, or someone your friends would appreciate you exposing them to.

Protecting Yourself

As with e-mail, blogs, discussion boards, or any other online communication, the first step to staying safe online with IM is to take the time to think about who you're communicating with and what information or images you are putting out there or opening yourself up to receive. Specifically, use these tips to become a safer IM user:

- Think about what you pick as a screen name and consider keeping it neutral. Don't give away personal information. Susie14smallville tells too much; pick something that doesn't help somebody identify or locate you.

- Consider who you want to communicate with via IM. Some people only want to communicate with close friends and family, and others use the service more openly. Decide what you are comfortable with and set appropriate limits. Remember that just because someone sends a request to you to be added to your contact list doesn't mean you want to or need to add them.

- Keep in mind that if someone has access to you through IM, they can also see your e-mail address.

- For younger children, limiting access to a safe list of buddies is advisable. Use a service that allows you to limit your child's contacts and allows you to get an overview of whom they are conversing with to ensure their safety. With teens, set boundaries that match your family's values and their age, and reassess the boundaries periodically as they mature. If the instant messaging program allows others to see your child's friends (called "friends of friends" functionality), and allows your child to be seen by all of his friend's friends, discuss what level of interaction is right for your situation and make sure the program settings reflect your comfort level. Hold a discussion with your kids about whom they communicate with and what they talk about. A good rule of thumb for anybody using IM is to not list your IM contact information publicly on blogs, discussion boards, social networking sites, and so on.

- Public computers—in libraries, Internet cafes, or even the computer at a friend's house—can pose a safety risk. Never select the feature that *automatically logs you on* to services and look to see that this is not the default on any machine you are using. When you log on to a public computer (or one that isn't your own) and it asks if you want to store your password or automatically log on, say "no." If you say "yes," the next person who logs on might be automatically signed in as you and have access to your account and your friends. Most likely, the next person to use the computer will just log off and open their own account, but they might not. If that person has ill intent, you will not only put yourself at risk, but also place all of your friends at risk. Imagine someone who wants to ruin your friendship by saying hurtful things while pretending to be you, or worse, somebody posing as you and asking your friend to meet somewhere. Your friend might go without realizing that she is actually meeting someone whose intentions are possibly dangerous.

- Not all IM features are appropriate for all ages. You should use features selectively with a clear understanding of how to use them safely. For example, some games might be more mature in content than is appropriate; you might want to decline voice and video interactions with people you haven't met; giving another person remote access to your computer should only be done when you have a specific problem that you want a trusted person to help you fix. Kids should never give their online friends remote access to a family computer.

- Be very cautious about meeting in person someone who you know only through IM. Everything they've told you about themselves and their motivation for meeting you might be completely true—or it could all be a lie. They might feel like a close friend, but they are still a stranger. If you do decide to meet an online-only contact, never go alone, make sure others know where you are going, and always have your cell phone handy.

- It is never safe to share sensitive personal information through unencrypted IM, and unless you know for sure that yours is encrypted, you should assume it is *not*. Never share passwords or credit card information over IM, for example.

Think About It

Look for a messaging provider that has good abuse-reporting and prevention tools. Many providers such as MSN/Windows Live are building more safety features into IM, and expanding their cooperation with authorities to stop abuses such as IM spam attacks, harassment, and illegal image distribution, as well as providing anti-virus protection services in their programs.

- Sharing photos and links in IM is an easy and convenient way to share with others, but while companies try hard to protect their IM users, spam and viruses can be a problem. To help keep your device safe from malicious attacks, don't open pictures, download files, or click links in messages from people you don't know. Sometimes links or photos might even look like they are sent by a friend, but if you aren't in the middle of a conversation when you get a file or link, double-check with the sender before you open anything. Remember that some viruses can automatically spread through your contact and buddy lists. Some types of content are always inappropriate and illegal. For example, it is illegal to possess or even view child pornography.

Think About It

If anyone sends you or your children inappropriate or illegal material, report it. Instruct your children not to shut down the computer but to turn off the monitor and walk away, and then to tell you as soon as possible. Tell your ISP and the police, if appropriate. Let the police instruct you about what to do with your computer to help them to collect evidence.

- Anything you say in IM can be forwarded to others—or monitored by employers if you use IM at work or on work machines. Consider what you are saying and how you would feel if the information were shared.

- Harassment and bullying can and do occur online. This is unacceptable behavior and in some cases can be illegal. Encourage your children to report such harassment to you. You can then, in turn, report harassment or abuse to your ISP and law enforcement if appropriate.

Find Out More

Chapter 16, "Step 13: Act to Avoid Harassment and Bullying," discusses the problem of online harassment and bullying and how to avoid it.

- Make conscious choices about the information you give away. Consider who can see this information. If both close friends and not-so-close friends or a network of friends of friends can view your profile or messages, you might want to be more conservative in showing emotions or saying that you're on vacation, as these can be useful pieces of information to people who want to exploit you or your property.

Figure 8-2 shows two examples of IM profiles. The IM profile on the left identifies the subject only to those who know him, while the one on the right reveals too much personal information.

Figure 8-2 Two examples of instant message profiles

If you think of IM as being like holding a quick conversation on a street corner, you'll probably make good choices about who to talk to, what to tell them, and whether you want that person to be able to follow you home or to a friend's house. Don't let the anonymity of an online text message make you forget that there is a person on the other end who might be a friend or a foe.

CHAPTER NINE

Step 6: Reduce Your Vulnerability When Blogging

Caroline's family had just moved to a new town, and she missed her friends in Brisbane. She decided that a great way to keep in touch would be to start a blog. All the kids at her new school were getting into blogging, so it would be a good way to make new friends, too.

Caroline found the sign-up process for her site easy to work through. Eager to get started, she accepted all the default settings and typed in her city and state in Australia. She thought that a racy nickname might make the kids at her new school think she was cool, so she chose "NaughtyCaroline." She entered her contact information and customized her Web address using her last name and the year she was born so she could remember it easily.

Caroline tried to make the background of her site look impressive (like many 14-year-old girls, she loves hearts and hot pink) and added a bunch of photos of herself and her friends with labels identifying them and the scenery in the photos. She also created a list of her favorite songs and posted it to the site.

Her new friend Amy came over to look at the site one Saturday morning and said it still looked kind of empty. Together the girls downloaded and filled out a few quizzes, challenging each other to come up with more and more outrageous answers. One survey asked how many beers she drinks in a week, and Amy taunted Caroline to say a dozen. In fact, Caroline doesn't drink at all, but she wants Amy to think she's sophisticated, so she entered 12 for her answer.

Over the next week, Caroline made lots of journal entries, finding that it was liberating to write about herself. In one entry, she mentioned her most recent fight with her mother, and admitted to being kind of lonely since she and Nigel broke up. She added that she's hoping to meet a "hot guy" when her family goes on vacation in Perth next week. Now that her blog isn't looking so empty, Caroline sends an instant message to her old and new friends telling them to check out her site.

She doesn't know that several online predators have already seen her site and are already getting to know her—really well.

What Just Happened?

Caroline just did something more common than you'd expect: she created her own blog without a clue about the safety risks. She didn't stop to consider that the default setting for her site is "viewable by the public" and that anyone with Internet access can see everything she's shared, including

- Her name
- Her friends' names
- Her family members' names
- Pictures of herself and others
- Where she lives
- Where she goes to school
- That she's lonely and fighting with her mother
- That their house will be empty next week

It never occurred to Caroline that anyone other than her friends can read her blog, that her information is now searchable by Internet search engines, or that she might have placed herself, her family, her home, her friends, and her possessions in harm's way.

Let me be clear about this: There is nothing at all "bad" about public blogs or other publicly posted content as long as you consider and make a clear decision about what you feel is appropriate to share with the public. There are literally millions of wonderful public blogs that are not placing their authors at any risk. But if you share personally identifying information about yourself or others, you should do so with a full understanding that this could easily be used by others.

Find Out More

See Chapter 17, "Talking About Safety," for information about how to create a family discussion guide to set parameters for online behavior in your family.

What Is a Blog?

Blogs, short for *Web logs*, first appeared when journalists in remote places wanted to post stories and commentary about their war-time experiences that they couldn't get out through other communication channels. Blogs then went mainstream, becoming personal online journals where entries could be posted by the blog owner and comments added by those visiting the blog. This frequent updating and interaction makes blogs much more dynamic than most Web sites. Each blog entry usually contains a title, a profile of the author, a date stamp, photos, and the poster's comments. They might also contain lists of favorite music and books, maps, videos, search tools, quizzes, and so on. Businesses and organizations have also jumped on the blogging bandwagon to offer information-rich sites that encourage interaction among their readers or users.

Blogs are social networking sites (Web sites that connect people and allow them to communicate with each other) *if* the blog owner includes contacts in the blog so that visitors (select friends and family or the public) can communicate with those people and thereby extend their networks.

Assessing the Risks

Blogs offer an environment where people can share their ideas and feelings with friends and family or with others who have similar interests, or even with the public at large. They encourage creativity, expression, and interaction. Blogs enable people to get involved and have a voice in politics and news reporting and other forms of participatory citizenship. They enable people to meet new friends and expand their horizons. So what makes people anxious about blogs?

The Blogging Phenomenon

There are more than 70 million blogs online today (*www.blogherald.com*). I've talked about blogs frequently throughout this book, in part because they are a relatively new tool for the general public and have become a wildly popular trend that is often in the headlines, usually because of abuses.

Unfortunately, a small segment of the population uses blogs in hurtful and illegal ways. Predators and bullies use the information that was intended to allow expression and inspire contact to spam, con, stalk, harass, and groom victims of every age. In a microcosm, blogging reinforces the point that anything new and popular, such as the Internet itself, poses problems in part just because it is new. People simply haven't learned about the potential risks and don't know how to blog safely.

Criminals and Blogs

As I mentioned in Chapter 1, "The Landscape of Risk," about half of all those who blog use their blogs as a form of emotional therapy. Because the blog format often is geared toward enabling people to reveal their attitudes, feelings, and personal information in a public way, they are attracting predators and criminals who hunt for the emotionally vulnerable or unwary. As in the real world, where you're advised against looking distracted or passive when walking alone, projecting an emotionally vulnerable face to the general public in a blog is an invitation to cybercriminals and predators.

Think About It

According to WiredSafety (*www.wiredsafety.org*), in 2005 about one-third of students in the United States had Internet blogs, although only about 5 percent of parents were aware of that fact.

Remember, the creators of the Internet didn't invent criminals or predators. The people who commit crimes online are the same people who commit crimes in the physical world. The Internet and the services enabled by it, such as blogs and social networks, are just new tools for them to use.

The Information Connection

All types of cybercriminals leverage information posted online to help them identify opportunities. Identity thieves look for identifying information, robbers look for items to steal, scam artists target people who seem susceptible to scams, and sexual predators search for victims. Middlemen aid these criminals by building catalogs of people and items that might be of interest: information about children, identities, addresses of homes whose owners are away, and locations of valuable cars. A lot of the leveraged information is gleaned from publicly accessible blogs, where people unthinkingly post all kinds of data about themselves.

While much of this information is provided by the victims themselves, sometimes it is unintentionally provided by friends or family members. It is the cybercriminal's ability to find *in one place* pieces of information that have been left over time by multiple people that gives him or her an advantage over other criminals, who have no such repository of information to sift through.

What You Expose About Yourself and Others

Bloggers expose their information in a variety of forms—from text descriptions of their feelings to photos and videos, music preferences, voice clips, lists of favorites, and maps.

A blog's topics can also reveal personal information. For example, adult and older bloggers are often interested in their family tree and genealogy research and frequently post all this information online (see Figure 9-1 on the next page), providing full names, mother's maiden name (a frequent password prompt used by online sites and financial institutions), birth dates, locations, marriage information, and so on, going back several generations. This is an identity thief's dream come true.

Information can also be discerned from a blog's background motif, a blogger's nickname, a Web URL (www.blogsite.Cecil24livin'thelifein-Victoria or www.blogsite.RobWalters26, for example), emoticons displayed, quotes, address field information, relationship status, or a biography. Figure 9-2 on page 77 shows a typical blog that provides a lot of information about its owner and is publicly posted.

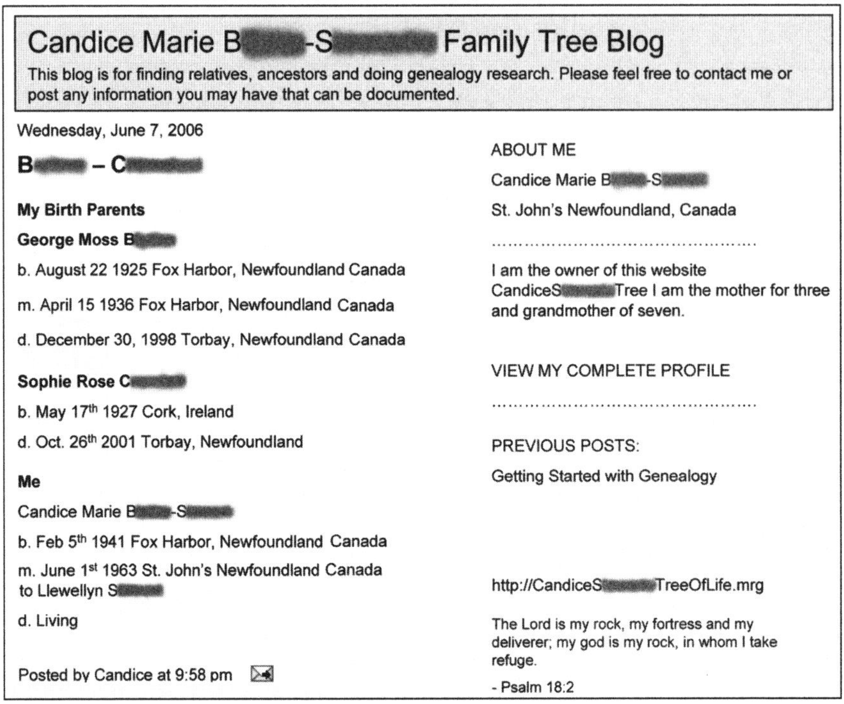

Candice Marie B██████-S████████ Family Tree Blog

This blog is for finding relatives, ancestors and doing genealogy research. Please feel free to contact me or post any information you may have that can be documented.

Wednesday, June 7, 2006

B█████ – C██████

My Birth Parents

George Moss B██████

b. August 22 1925 Fox Harbor, Newfoundland Canada

m. April 15 1936 Fox Harbor, Newfoundland Canada

d. December 30, 1998 Torbay, Newfoundland Canada

Sophie Rose C█████

b. May 17th 1927 Cork, Ireland

d. Oct. 26th 2001 Torbay, Newfoundland

Me

Candice Marie B█████-S██████

b. Feb 5th 1941 Fox Harbor, Newfoundland Canada

m. June 1st 1963 St. John's Newfoundland Canada to Llewellyn S██████

d. Living

Posted by Candice at 9:58 pm ✉

ABOUT ME

Candice Marie B█████-S██████

St. John's Newfoundland, Canada

....

I am the owner of this website CandiceS██████Tree I am the mother for three and grandmother of seven.

VIEW MY COMPLETE PROFILE

....

PREVIOUS POSTS:

Getting Started with Genealogy

http://CandiceS██████TreeOfLife.mrg

The Lord is my rock, my fortress and my deliverer; my god is my rock, in whom I take refuge.
- Psalm 18:2

Figure 9-1 A genealogy blog

Many people provide contact information, such as IM and e-mail accounts, phone numbers, and full street addresses. Many bloggers fill out one of the myriad surveys people can post about themselves, thinking that a flirty answer about their personal life is just fun, until a predator latches on to their answer and targets his next victim. Surveys and profiles are particularly high-risk collections of information. I found answers such as these to a survey on a 17-year-old girl's site (I've inserted the categories of answers):

- **Drugs**

  I've tried marijuana.

  I have passed out drunk in the past six months.

- **Sex**

  I go for older guys/girls, not younger.

- **Emotional health**

  I have changed a lot mentally over the last year.

I fall for the worst people and have been hurt every time.

I have been intentionally hurt by people that I loved.

- **Self-esteem**

  I don't like it when people are unpleased or seem unpleased with me.

- **Identifiers**

  I have long hair.

  I have lived in either three different states or countries (MA, ID, AK).

  I have at least one sibling.

- **Internet usage**

  I have more friends on the Internet than in real life.

  I'm online 24/7.

  I like surveys.

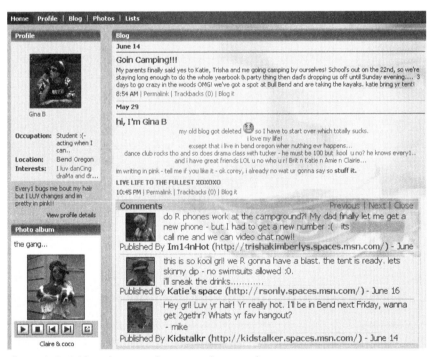

Figure 9-2 A blog that reveals too much to predators

Find Out More

Find out about the risks of sharing information in Chapter 5, the risks of sharing photos and other visual clues in Chapter 4, and how predators prey on the emotionally vulnerable in Chapter 6. For information about the risks involved in blogging when you're grieving, refer to *www.look-both-ways.com*.

Who's Most at Risk?

According to David Huffaker's analysis and FBI data, at particularly high risk are young people between the ages of 13 and 15, when they make their blogs available to the public instead of to a limited group of friends and family. This is a time when teens are reaching out for new identities, friends, and validation. At the same time, they are often struggling with their existing relationships with their current friends, with their girlfriend or boyfriend, with family members (especially parents), and with teachers, as well as with their own unstable emotions.

Also at higher risk are young people who live in rural areas or suburbs (Wolak et al., 2004). They have a greater need to meet new people (they probably already know everyone in town) and tend to be more trusting of strangers than are kids in urban environments.

When Spam Meets Blog: Spam + Blog = Splog

If you allow the public to leave comments on your blog, you have opened the door to another rapidly increasing phenomenon, spam on blogs. Called "**splog**," this involves placing a comment, link, or graphic on your site that encourages you and anyone viewing your blog to visit the spam author's own blog or some commercial site. Of course, when you get there, you find that you're viewing an advertisement for anything from a gambling site to a pornography site. Or you discover that someone is trying to cheat the system and increase their blog's popularity for some reason—possibly because they are getting a revenue share from advertisers based on how many people they can attract to their site.

But people of any age who are looking for new friends, have low self-esteem, or who are suffering from depression, grieving, or otherwise emotionally vulnerable are also likely victims. In less than nine minutes on average, I can locate adults, as well as teens, through the information they've put in their public blogs. Ironically, some of the worst examples of adults providing too much information in public blogs are individuals whose jobs are computer related. Although they might be confident techsperts (technical + expert = techspert) who can avoid technical issues such as viruses and spyware, they are often no more likely to understand human predators and the risks they pose than the average 13-year-old.

Protecting Yourself

Blogs, when open to the public, are often the intersection of several sets of potential pitfalls I've explored in previous chapters in this book. The specific advice in Chapters 4 through 7 on mitigating those risks should be applied to your own blogging activity. In addition to that advice, this section provides recommendations to help you blog more safely.

Don't Overreact

How do you advise your children if you feel they have placed themselves, your family, or their friends at risk? One of the most common reactions parents have when they read about abuses of people through public blogs is to want to stop their child from blogging altogether. While that is an option—and perhaps an appropriate option if a child is very young—for most kids this is simply not practical, nor particularly helpful.

Kids can access the Internet and blog from their friends' computers and many cell phones today, and the ability to blog from commonly available devices will only increase. Instead of cutting them off from the tremendous opportunities blogging affords, you should focus on teaching them *how to blog safely.*

Find Out More

See Chapter 17 for information about how to start a dialog and create a family discussion guide.

Knowing How Information Adds Up

Most people (but far from all) are cautious about putting *all* their information in their blog profile. But what people don't realize is that the information they provide usually compounds over time. Here's an example of how this works:

David creates a blog and enters his city and state, first name, and age. He posts a few photos of himself with family and friends. That's a big chunk of personal information and introduces *some* risk, but he talked this over with his folks and they decided they were fine with it.

- A friend comments on one of his photos and refers to David by his last name: "Hey M----- (I'm disguising the last name here, but his friend did not), great photo."

  A predator now has a full name, identifying photo, age, and city and state, and might well be able to use a white pages listing to pinpoint David as one of seven M------s living in Williamsburg, Virginia. In addition, because mapping technologies allow you to plot multiple locations on a map, the predator can begin tightening the web of location information to zero in on David's house.

- David posts a blog talking about his science lab at school. He also notes that he is in a bad mood because he got dumped by Jacqueline. Though he deserved it, he still feels crummy.

  David has exposed an emotional vulnerability. Anyone scanning the blog knows David might be looking for a new girlfriend. An easy way to approach him is with a fake picture of a cute girl who thinks he's "wonderful." Rarely do boys resist providing access to their blog to a "cute girl" who is interested in them. Of course, it might not be David the predator is interested in; it could be his 6-year-old sister Sarah who is in his photo album, or his 9-year-old brother Adam, or both.

- A second friend leaves a comment that he'll watch him in next Tuesday's game and meet him at the side gate after—"Go Titans!"

  A quick Web search on high school football teams in Williamsburg provides David's school name so David can be easily located (a predator has the place, date, and time of the game and his photo). This information also corroborates that David's age and city information were accurately entered and not faked. The school location eliminates four of the last-named "M-----s" in town from the potential list because they live within other school districts. The search is now down to three likely houses.

- In a blog entry the next day, David talks about going fishing in the river and tells Ben and Tom to meet him at the dock behind his house and gives driving directions.

  David is now locatable both at school and at home, and he's made his house a good target for theft. It's a safe bet his house will be empty during the ballgame because his folks will probably attend. A robber now has a great opportunity. David's picture and identity information could be used to create a phony passport or a fake ID.

> **Think About It**
>
> People who post on social networks would reduce their risks considerably if they didn't leave all their postings, photos, and other material out there forever. It is very easy to leak a few drops of information here and there into a large online bucket. That wouldn't be such a big deal if the bucket were emptied occasionally.

Taking Steps for Safety

The first step to protecting yourself and your family is to have a solid understanding of what kinds of information risks there are, how information might get exposed, and what you can do to mitigate or avoid the risks.

> **Think About It**
>
> There are several sites that blatantly push users into revealing a great deal of personal information about themselves publicly, telling them that nobody will visit their space unless they put interesting details in their profile or that posting their pictures will get more new friends to visit their blog. This is entirely irresponsible. Know the attitude toward safety and the privacy policy of any site before using it.

Beyond basic awareness, here's a checklist of advice to help make your blogging safer:

- Make a conscious choice when setting up access to your blog. Most blog sites have several options, ranging from a personal journal that only you can see, to a site open to a defined group of friends and family, to a site available to a looser group of friends and their friends, all the way to a completely public site accessible to anyone in the world. Unfortunately, most sites default to a "publicly viewable" option, and you have to make an effort to look for the other options.

- If you want to share your blog with a larger group that includes people who do not know you personally or make your blog public, consider archiving older material so there is no accumulation of information. Review your blog postings periodically with a view toward understanding how much information you have made available as content and comments begin to accumulate.

- Choose a user name that is not suggestive or revealing. Your name should also not reveal your age, location, or gender.

- Be careful what you divulge through text and don't be recognizable through your photos (see Figure 9-3 for an example of a photo that isn't too revealing). Also, be aware what you might give away in a photo label. All too often users place clearly identifying information in photo captions that give themselves and their friends or family away, such as "Nigel and Kate in Kingsbridge on Saturday." If you want to post identifying images, you should strongly consider more restricted access to your site.

Figure 9-3 This blogger's photo doesn't show her appearance too clearly.

- Monitor your friends' comments so you are not exposed through them. The example shown in Figure 9-4 reveals how quickly friends' comments expose others. In this example, these three friends completely exposed the blog owner and themselves.

- Encourage your children to come to you if somebody who comments on their blog makes them feel uncomfortable in any way— whether that person is a friend, a family member, or a stranger.

- Be cautious about what you include in your profile and recognize that some blog and social networking sites make your profile contents publicly available and searchable, even if your blog itself is private.

Figure 9-4 Taken together, all this information reveals a lot about these kids and the blog's owner.

- Make sure the blogging site you use has clear privacy and security policies, provides tools for protection, and is responsive to reports of abuse.

- According to international ethnography research as well as industry research, for many teens, more buddies equals increased social status. Don't add people you don't know to a buddy list if you are sharing personal information, and don't include people on your buddy list unless you feel comfortable about who they are. Remember: If you don't recognize the buddy name and the person has not requested contact with you in your comments area, the comment is quite likely spam.

- Don't play blog exposé. To get repeat attention teens will often get more and more risqué in their content and pictures. The potential for harm even within extended friend and family groups increases as the site gets racier and more personal.

- Finally, talk to your family and your friends. Everyone you interact with online needs to work together if you are to help each other learn your way around this new online world.

Think About It

Often people feel safer about receiving comments from and responding to some-body who lives far away, assuming they can't get at them. Keep in mind, however, that people can say they are located anywhere they want. They might live exactly where they claim to live, or they might live much, much closer.

Be Aware of What Your Friends Are Saying About You

One final point to keep in mind is that you are not the only one putting your information online through blogs. *Your risk level is based on what your collective group is saying about you, not just what you say.* It's vital that you share the cautions contained in this book with your friends and family and be aware of what they are putting online.

Here are the key steps for working with your family and friends to keep all of you safe:

- **Posting photos of others, or text that provides information about others in any way, without their knowledge and permission is disrespectful and might well be illegal.** It isn't okay to provide a friend's last name, their birthday, or where you're going to meet them, unless both parties agree that they want that information posted. This shows disrespect for their right to choose the level of exposure they are comfortable with. You should not only ask per-mission, but you should also make it clear who can see your site. In the case of minors, you might need to get their parents' permission.

- **Discuss your comfort level with sharing information that locates you.** If your social networking site is conservative and doesn't provide personal information that would help locate you but your friend's site does, then your information is still public. Take the time to browse through a couple of your friends' blogs to see what they say about you. If a friend tells what school they attend and there is a comment that you two have a class together, a suggestion to meet out front after school, or a remark about a favorite teacher, it doesn't matter that you didn't provide your school information. Your friend just did it for you.

- **Keep in mind that "friends" can be a very fluid concept.** Both you and your friends will meet new people and shift friendships throughout your lives. At some point you might just drift away (jobs change, schools change, interests change), or you might experience a rift that suddenly breaks the friendship. How will your information be treated then? Occasionally you should review who has access to your site and make changes if necessary.

- You might have two friends who don't like each other. You don't want your blog to become the middle ground in a battle between your friends. Perhaps they've had a falling out or perhaps they never liked each other. What agreements are you making with each of them that will provide the level of safety the other needs?

- **Permissions can change.** Either you or a friend might, at a later date (even tomorrow), decide to change the permissions on your sites. How will your/their information be treated if the permissions on their site become public? Will your information be removed or archived? Will it be maintained in a section that is only for limited viewers (where some information is viewable by the public and some is set to private)? Or will your information get the same level of exposure as the rest of the site and suddenly become much more public than you had intended?

- **If you want your blog to be a social networking site, keep in mind that your level of safety from exposure is only as strong as the weakest link in your social network chain.** Even if you and your friends have agreed about avoiding exposure, you probably don't have such an agreement with all of *their friends*. Although you might ask your friend not to tell people what school *you* go to, if your friend posts a comment about *his* school and mentions your name, a predator can assume it's pretty likely that you all go to the same school. There is a potential for information to leak several tiers out in the network and eventually identify you.

As you apply the age-old social network infrastructure to your new virtual world, you have to be careful to look both ways and consider all the potential hazards to be able to get around safely.

CHAPTER TEN

Step 7: Understand Risks of Fraudulent Communications and Protect Yourself

Hal finished eating his frozen pizza and headed for his computer in the corner of the living room. He was waiting for an e-mail message from his friend Steve, who was sending him some strategies for the computer game they were going to play tonight.

As the time approached for their game, Hal checked his e-mail. There were two messages from Steve in the inbox. There were also six messages that seemed to have been sent by Hal but had bounced back to his account as undeliverable, and all of them had the same subject line, "Be A Hit w/Girls." He'd never sent out anything like that. Curious, he clicked on one and scanned the undelivered message. It had been sent out to somebody in the United Kingdom he'd never heard of. Hal was horrified as he realized the message was offering male sex "aids" using his e-mail address as the sender.

"Geez!" Hal said while deleting the messages, humiliated that his account might have been used in a method called spoofing to sell sex toys to thousands of people. Even as he was cursing the person who had used him in this way, the e-mail recipients were probably cursing his name and assuming he was the spammer. He'd heard about this, but this was the first time he was a victim.

After deleting the spoofed e-mail messages, Hal, trying to calm down, turned his attention to the e-mail from Steve. The first message's subject line read "just for you"; the second had no title at all. Hal, not wanting to be caught twice in one night, assumed the message with no subject might be bogus, so he clicked on the one titled "just for you." He was furious when he realized he'd been fooled again. What he saw was yet another piece of spam with a pornographic image, lurid text, and a link to a Web site that provided more of the same.

Hal clicked the "report junk mail" icon on his monitor screen so hard he almost broke his mouse. "It's getting so you just don't want to go online any-more," he mumbled to himself.

What Just Happened?

Hal is a technically savvy guy, but that doesn't make him immune to e-mail and other communication delivery method abuses such as spoof-ing and spam. Spoofers can use his legitimate e-mail address to help them bypass spam filters. The messages they are sending are sometimes illegal and can range from annoying to offensive. In addition, a friend like Steve might download a virus that forwards a message to his entire contact list, or Steve himself might have been a spoofing victim. Fortunately, Hal was smart enough not to click any links or open any file attachments sent through the spam messages.

No matter how such spam messages are sent on, about 30 percent of users admit to not always knowing if an e-mail message is spam, and many don't know how to deal with spam. Spam messages, such as the e-mail Hal received, are sent by the *billions* every day, and although the vast majority are caught by your ISP's spam filter, some do get through. Choosing an e-mail provider that uses e-mail authentication, like Sender ID, can help. Ask your provider what protections they have. Be sure to report fraudulent spam messages, and don't buy anything from the ads.

What Is Spoofing?

Spoofing involves capturing, modifying, and retransmitting an online communication so that the recipient is led to believe it is from someone other than the actual sender.

What Is Spam?

Spam e-mail is sent in bulk to recipients who have not requested it, from senders they usually do not know. Spam is a cheap way to market products or services and apparently is a successful sales tool.

Spam differs from legitimate direct marketing via e-mail where the recipient has agreed to receive mail from the sender. Spam is illegal in many countries and for good reason. It can be transmitted over any Internet-connected device.

Assessing the Risks

In addition to the huge annoyance factor, spam undermines your confidence in e-mail and opens you up to many fraudulent ploys. One FTC report indicated that 66 percent of spam contained "false or misleading information in the sender line, subject line, or message content."

Spam also drives enormous costs on to service providers who have to gear up to handle the billions of spam communications sent daily. Development teams have to constantly create new rules to try to block the deluge in a seemingly never-ending cycle as spammers find new holes to crawl through. For example, MSN Hotmail blocks over 3.2 billion spam messages every day. Over 90 percent of incoming messages are spam, and Hotmail's filtering processes catch over 95 percent of those spam messages.

While the battle against e-mail spam rages on, the problem is spreading to new services and devices. Spam plagues mobile communications and any Internet service through which users can be contacted. Spam is found on classified advertising and auction sites and is posted in chat rooms, on discussion boards, in IM and blogs (as mentioned in the last two chapters), and more.

Find Out More

For more information about risks you can avoid while instant messaging, see Chapter 8, "Step 5: Don't Expose Yourself Through Instant Messaging." To learn more about ways to protect yourself while blogging, see Chapter 9, "Step 6: Reduce Your Vulnerability When Blogging."

Telltale Signs of Spam Scams

Here are some telltale signs that identify an e-mail scam:

- You don't know the sender of the message.

- You are promised untold sums of money for little or no effort on your part.

- You are asked to provide money and/or information up front for questionable activities, to provide a processing fee, or to pay the cost of expediting the process.

- You are asked to provide or verify your bank account number or other personal financial information, even if the sender offers to deposit money into your account.

- It looks like it comes from a bank or company you know and asks you to click on a link to their site or respond to the e-mail to validate information.

- The request contains a sense of urgency.

- The sender repeatedly requests confidentiality.

- The sender offers to send you photocopies of government certificates, banking information, or other "evidence" that their activity is legitimate.

- The subject line looks compelling or suggests that the message is in response to some action you took, such as placing an order or requesting an insurance quote.

Spammers are smart. They know how to pique your curiosity, flatter you, and challenge you. No matter the effect, if it gets you to open the e-mail and respond in some way, they win.

Facing the Fraud

Different people fall for different types of scams, so these messages might announce that "you've won" a sweepstakes or some other prize. Or they might look like an official survey that asks your opinion. Once you've answered the questions, they throw in a few more about age, address, and income bracket. Or they use any other likely hook that can reel you in.

Even the cleverest people might fall prey to an e-mail scam, so it's worth knowing some of the typical ploys so you can spot them when they land in your inbox.

Here are some popular e-mail scams to be aware of:

- Some bulk e-mail displays links that look like they will take you to one Web site, but actually take you to another. This ploy could cause you to enter sign-in information for your bank's site, ISP, or an online auction or payment site. In fact, you have actually landed on a cleverly disguised but phony site, called a phishing site, run by a criminal hoping to capture your information.

Find Out More

To learn more about phishing and other financial scams, see Chapter 14, "Step 11: Get Savvy About Financial Scams and Fraud."

- E-mail urban legends are also on the rise. They might simply hook you into forwarding a startling "news" story to everybody you know, or ask you to take other actions. There are actually urban legend Web sites, such as *www.snopes.com, www.urbanlegends.about.com,* and *www.hoaxbusters.ciac.org,* where you can check whether an e-mail message you received presents factual information or a fictionalized version of information presented as fact. The goal for the original sender is often to increase the size of their distribution lists both for themselves and for the resale value of e-mail addresses on the open market.

- Free rarely means free. These free product offers usually turn out to be pyramid schemes that require you to earn points toward your "free" product by providing personal information and by getting other people to join the scheme.

Communicating Safely

When you communicate using e-mail, you open a channel for communication just like you do when you turn on your cell phone. To protect yourself from harassing or annoying e-mail, and from revealing your location or other personal information through your e-mail, be aware of the following issues.

- What is your e-mail address telling about you? In choosing an e-mail address, you might be giving away information about yourself you don't really want to share with everybody to whom you send an e-mail. People often choose their own name or a name that includes their school or town, or identifies gender, for example. This is useful not only to spammers, but to a whole host of cybercriminals.

- **E-mail signatures** at the bottom of your messages are a handy way to include your contact information when communicating with people you know. These typically provide your full name, often a work title, an address, and a home phone, cell phone, and fax number. However, if they are inserted automatically in all your e-mail responses, you might unwittingly reveal more information than you intended to share with people you don't know. How they choose to use that information is up to them.

Think About It

Sexual predators quite often convince children to provide their e-mail addresses so they can communicate with them on a regular basis and share things such as identifying pictures or pornography. These people might also teach the children how to erase any record of e-mail sent to or received from the predator.

Protecting Yourself

E-mail and other forms of online messaging are terrific communication tools that let you exchange information with coworkers and clients, transmit files and pictures, and stay in touch with friends and family. But always be careful about what mail you open, especially if there are attachments or inserted graphics, and what information you send out. To help promote your safety, many e-mail providers will strip out attachments and graphics when they cannot verify the legitimacy of the attachments.

Taking the First Steps

So what can you do about spam? Here are four steps that can help to protect you from the negative effects of spam:

- First, set your e-mail service's spam filters to a high setting (review the settings to find what works best for you). You'll then need to check your junk e-mail folder periodically to see if a potentially legitimate e-mail message was somehow blocked. If it was, you might want to add the legitimate e-mail address to your list of approved senders to avoid this in the future. Your e-mail provider can give you instructions on how to do this if you are unsure.

- Second, never respond to a spam message. While it may be very tempting to respond to the spammer, if only to complain about the mail, it will likely not work. The e-mail account you send it to will rarely ever be legitimate, and you will have validated that your e-mail account is in fact legitimate and active, which can increase the amount of spam you get.

- Third, report spam to your e-mail provider. There should be an easy-to-find way for you to report spam in your e-mail inbox. The more you report, the better the spam filters will become at determining what should be blocked. You'll do yourself and hundreds of millions of other users a favor by reporting spam.

- Fourth, *never* buy something offered through a spam message. If no one purchased through this mechanism or was fooled by the scams that spam so often veils in get-rich-quick offers or phishing schemes, spam would not be lucrative and it would subside. Figure 10-1 on the next page shows an example of classic "storefront" spam.

You help perpetuate the problem when you respond to this type of e-mail and make it financially rewarding for these cybercriminals to operate. You also run a very high risk of exposing your personal and financial information.

Think About It

It's important that you understand the protective services that your e-mail provider makes available to you. Microsoft e-mail products, for example, provide spam filtering and automatic attachment scanning for viruses and malware.

Figure 10-1 A typical spam message

Avoiding Incoming Threats

Just as you toss away several pieces of unwanted paper mail every day, you also need to weed through e-mail to get rid of unwanted or potentially malicious messages. Here are some guidelines to help you swim through the sea of spam without sinking:

- No reputable company should send you e-mail telling you to follow a link to validate your account or personal information. If you get this kind of e-mail, it is surely an attempt at fraud. If you're ever in doubt or have any questions, call the number on your credit card or account statement. Do not call any number that might appear in that e-mail message, and notify the bank about the mail you received.

- Don't fall for flattery. Another angle for spam and stalkers is to flatter and express interest in you (see Figure 10-2). They leave the reference to when they met you vague and often send a photo of an attractive girl or guy, depending on who they are targeting. If you provide more information, agree to meet them, or open any attachment, you could fall victim to a scheme.

- Avoid clicking on links that are sent in e-mail. It is better to type the address into your browser yourself than to follow a link, or look up the company in a search engine and use that link to get to the site. If you must follow e-mail links, verify that the link takes you to where it says it does, and be very cautious about what information you enter. People can name a link anything, but where it actually takes you is another story. Remember that a destination URL can be cleverly disguised to look like another site.

- Consider using a secondary e-mail address as the address you provide for an online classified ad or to online dating contacts, for example. Until you can trust someone, don't expose your primary e-mail account address.

- If you want to unsubscribe from the e-mail sent to you from *legitimate* companies, you *do* need to use the unsubscribe functionality found at the bottom of their e-mail or go to the company's Web site and find their unsubscribe process.

From:	Pleeezze believe me (ifitsoundstoogoodtobetrue@thenitis.con)
Date:	Friday, August 11, 2006 5 PM
To:	Mynextvictim.con
Subject:	

I lovedyoursmile! You are a hotgurl and i am a really hotguy rich and friendly so we should get together. Why don't you give me your IM address or lookmeup my name there is studluv.

Meet methere tomorrow @ 4-8pm your time.

Djdidjhdlsjsuiendkflfhsuipeiemneisuosiwfkkruish

Ifitsoundstogoodtobetruethenitis

Figure 10-2 Don't be taken advantage of by false flattery.

Remember, if you stick to personal or business communications in e-mail and verify each sender, you are likely to stay safe. Respond to any sales pitch, get-rich-quick messages, account validation requests, or would-be admirers and you're taking a risk with both your finances and your identity.

CHAPTER ELEVEN

Step 8: Date Safely Online

Suzanne and her girlfriends had been talking about Internet dating for months, but nobody had the nerve to try it. One night while they were out together, the women decided it was time for one of them to go for it. They took a vote, and Suzanne was elected.

The following evening, Suzanne and her friend Michelle sat down to compose her listing. They agreed to post it for one month on a dating site with a good reputation, and to play it safe by creating a fake name and using an e-mail account provided by the service for replies. Before finalizing her personal ad, Suzanne uploaded a picture of herself from her college graduation party a year ago. She was wearing a short-sleeved top and shorts, smiling into the camera as her father took her picture in their backyard.

The next evening, Suzanne logged on to her online dating e-mail account to pick up any messages from prospective dates. A few were trashy and she deleted them immediately, relieved that she had given a fake name and was not using her regular e-mail address. One or two guys sounded intriguing, so she printed those messages to show Michelle.

As Suzanne continued to read messages, she came across one from a man who said he had been interested in her personal ad until he saw the pornographic personals she was posting on other dating sites. There was one with the name loads_of_fun_4_evry1, and another that said she was looking for "a good time" on the first date.

Suzanne called Michelle in a panic. Michelle came over and together they located the ads the man had mentioned. Mystified, the two young women stared at the innocent picture of Suzanne they had posted only the day before, now modified to show lots of bare skin. As they continued to search online, they discovered with a sinking feeling that Suzanne's modified photo was now posted all over the Internet.

"Oh, no," Suzanne moaned. "What will my parents say?"

What Just Happened?

According to the Identity Theft Resource Center, it's not uncommon for women to discover that their pictures are being used in some unsavory ways online. Their photos are modified using image-editing software, and then used to lure men into online chats that mask commercial pornography sites. Men are the intended financial victims of this type of fraud, but the women whose photos have been stolen and altered are also victims.

Internet dating is a terrific way for people to meet new friends, but Suzanne's case underscores one of the pitfalls of posting personal information online to find a date or a mate: Even when you take precautions and use reputable sites, there are still some risks.

Does that mean that online dating should be avoided at all costs? Certainly not. I personally know several women who are now married to wonderful partners they met through Internet dating sites, and chances are you do too.

> **Think About It**
>
> Many social networking sites now offer online dating services for free. However, you need to clearly understand any potential trade-offs, as these sites likely do not have the same safety precautions that established dating sites provide. These features include screening, separate communication accounts so you do not have to give access to your primary e-mail or IM account, and site monitoring for abuses.

Assessing the Risks

Online dating has become considerably more common in recent years. Among single Internet users looking for a partner, 37 percent have visited an online dating site. The majority of these people report having had a positive experience, according to Pew Internet & American Life Project research published in March 2006. Additionally, the report indicates that 31 percent of American adults say they know people who have used a dating site. About half of those people know someone who has been in a long-term relationship or who is married to a partner they met online.

Still, as with all other online activity, online dating requires you to be cautious and take steps to protect yourself. According to the same Pew Internet & American Life Project research, about 66 percent of Americans feel that online dating is dangerous (only 25 percent do not believe online dating is dangerous) because of the risks associated with placing personal information online. Indeed, as I've stated many times in this book, it is true that placing personal information in a publicly accessible location can pose risks that should be considered and mitigated.

To help minimize your risks, carefully research dating sites to find one that is a good match for you, does not make your information publicly available, has clear safety precautions, and provides users with safety advice. Then consider how your own actions might help protect you or expose you to more risk.

As illustrated in the opening story, one risk of online dating is having your photo stolen and used in ways you would never approve of. Having your photo stolen and abused can leave you feeling violated and humiliated. It can even pose a physical risk to you if someone who sees your faked image arranges to meet you and assumes that you will behave in the way the fake postings claim you do. Although reputable dating service providers are constantly on the lookout for this type of fraud and respond immediately to remove fake ads if you notify them, some dating sites are far less diligent. In addition, personals can be posted on other sites, such as online classifieds and blogs. In fact, at this point in time, I'm not aware of any dating site that provides countermeasures to prevent the copying of either your image or your text.

Think About It

Your photo can live online forever and come back to haunt you in many ways for years to come. Think carefully before posting personally identifiable or suggestive images for public viewing. While this alone will not guarantee that your picture isn't abused, the chances of that happening decrease substantially.

Photo theft is only one potential concern. Cybercriminals can often learn a great deal from a personal ad and a couple of online conversations. Many online daters provide enough information about themselves for anybody to locate them fairly quickly. This places daters at risk of robbery, identity theft, or physical assault. In Jansen's posting shown in Figure 11-1, anybody could get his full name, address, phone number, when his house will be empty, a physical description, and a clear sense of his values and biases.

The goal of successful online dating is to eventually meet offline, which comes with the trade-off of losing your online anonymity. Be cautious about putting yourself at risk by offering too much information too soon, or proceeding to an offline relationship too quickly. Always follow your instincts: If you feel like someone is moving too quickly or asking for too much personal information, shut off the communication.

Category: People > Men Seeking Women

SWM seeks female near Laurel
Age: 35
Location: ███████ Mississippi   View map
Zip/Postal Code: 39440

Description:

My name is Jansen K. R███ and I live at 1365 Old Bay Springs Rd. in ███████ Mississippi. I am 35, 6'2" high, and 215lbs. I am certain that I have no children and I do live alone in a two story/brick home that I own.

I have bluegreen eyes and brown hair. I work fulltime as a contractor and have weekends off. My email is jankr███@hotmail.com. If you are interested call me at ███ ███ ████. I don't chat online and I don't allow smoking in my house. I am interested in your pics. Sorry no pics of me available as my skimpy computer is not capable.

Figure 11-1 Many online daters give away lots of information very quickly.

The way that free sites (especially teen dating sites) make money is usually through advertising and gathering and selling data, a practice called data mining. They are therefore highly motivated to encourage you to return to the site often and to get you to provide information. Because of this, some sites push you to reveal considerably more than you should (see Figure 11-2). If you choose to not leave a photo of yourself, you might receive a message such as "People who don't post photos don't get very many dates." Or, if you prefer not to enter as much personal information as is being asked for, you might see text that tells you "Enter enough information to make yourself sound exciting to a potential partner." Some of these sites also have extremely broad ideas about appropriate dating ranges, such as "14 years old to 45 years old"!

Add photo

Create a photo caption (Optional short description of photo)

☐ Rate me! Am I hot?   [100] Characters remaining

[Browse...]   *Profiles with photos get clicked on 5 times*
as often as those without a photo

Basic stuff about you

First Name	Last Name Name

Age ▾   Ethnic Background ▾   In a relationship? ▾

City ▾   State ▾

Who's your match?   **Your ideal age range**   **Their location**

Male – Female - Both? ▾   13 ▾ ↓   45 ▾ ↑   (Miles from you) ▾

Ethnic Background ▾   20 Miles
50 Miles
75 Miles
I don't care

Your interests.. (put a ✓ in boxes that match your style)
If you don't tell, how will we know who to match you with? Don't be shy....

Fashion: (✓ all that apply)
☐ I'm a clotheshorse
☐ I don't have a style
☐ Total Emo
☐ Latest trends only *dahling*
☐ Black.
☐ I'd rather be naked

What's your mood: (✓ all that apply)
☐ Completely depressed
☐ Out of control
☐ Angry
☐ Please make me feel better
☐ Just call me sunshine
☐ Depends on the drugs

R u Naughty? (✓ all that apply)
☐ Skinny dipped
☐ Passed out drunk
☐ Cheated on your girl/boyfriend
☐ Taken Drugs
☐ Shoplifted
☐ Got in a fight

R u a friend-magnet: (✓all that apply)
☐ I don't have friends
☐ I have a few close friends
☐ I'm so-so on the social scale
☐ I hate most people
☐ I fit in a couple of crowds
☐ Everyone loves me – super popular

[Tell more... >>]   [Find a match >>]

Figure 11-2 Typical methods to convince you to share more than you should

Protecting Yourself

A little prevention can come between you and heartache or even physical danger when it comes to online dating. To protect yourself while looking for a partner online, consider following these guidelines:

- **Select your online dating company carefully.** Look for an established, popular site with plenty of members and a philosophy that matches your own, as different sites cater to different audiences. Popularity can be a good indicator that a dating service is keeping members happy and safe. Spend time evaluating their tools and policies for online safety. Some sites conduct a background screening, but do not feel lulled into safety by this claim. Standards vary for what is included in a background check, and cybercriminals might slip past even the best of these. And never use a site that doesn't provide an easy way for you to report problems or that doesn't take appropriate action when notified of a problem.

- **Maintain anonymity to protect your identity.** Don't include your full name, phone number, where you work, or detailed location information in your profile or during early communications with potential dates. Leverage the e-mail system provided by the dating service to create a separate e-mail account. If you do choose to use your regular e-mail (which I don't recommend), turn off your e-mail signature feature and be sure that your e-mail address does not provide information about you. Make a conscious choice about the image you are projecting in your e-mail alias or account name. BostonSailor, skilovrUtah, or words such as foxy, flirty, sexy, hopeful, waiting, and so on, say things about you that you might not have intended.

Think About It

You are probably so used to signing e-mail and letters with your real name that it is easy to forget to protect your identity when communicating with a potential date. Take your time when you write, and you'll be less likely to make this mistake.

- **Be smart about choosing profile pictures.** Make sure your photos reflect what you want to say about yourself. Many people post provocative pictures and then are surprised by undesirable responses. Also ensure that your images do not contain identifying information, such as landmarks, a beer can from a local brewery, or a T-shirt with your company logo. If anybody presses you for identifiable information before you are ready to share it, consider that a warning flag.

- **Check to see if a potential date has a reputation among other daters on the service.** It isn't foolproof, but could provide some insight about a potential date. If the reputation isn't rock solid, move on.

- **Proceed carefully and always trust your instincts.** Be slow to trust anybody you meet online. Keep in mind that you don't have to provide your last name, address, or phone number to meet somebody for an in-person date. Don't paint a picture of your life in the first e-mail: Give people enough information to know what you're about but not so much that they can learn who you are. Trust your gut feelings if somebody seems too good to be true. Don't build a fantasy around a photo that might or might not be real. Look for danger signs such as displays of anger, frustration, disrespect, or any attempt to control you. If somebody fails to answer direct questions or provides inconsistent information about their looks, job, marital status, and so on, walk away and report this to the site. Keep in mind that it is not only women who get stalked and harassed, or whose homes get robbed while they are on a date.

Think About It

While communicating with online date candidates, consider blocking caller ID on your phone or use a cell phone that can't be easily traced to your address.

- **When in doubt, slow down.** You don't want to date anyone who doesn't respect your need to feel safe about your choices.

- **You have the right to walk away at any time.** You don't have to explain, apologize, or reply to a follow-up e-mail if you decide to walk away. Most dating sites have a feature that allows you to block the person from contacting you if you want communication to stop (a great reason to leverage the site's e-mail system and not use your own account name).

- **When you decide to meet, create a safe environment.** Keep first dates short (lunch is a good idea), and agree to meet in a public place during a busy time of day. Avoid any activity that leaves you alone, such as a hike or drive. Make sure somebody knows where you're going. If you do move to another location, call first to notify others of your plans. Always bring a cell phone and schedule a check-in with a friend or family member. If your date doesn't look like his or her photo, walk away and report it to the dating service. If they lie about their looks, they might lie about other things. Use your own transportation; never accept a ride. If you feel unsafe, don't apologize; excuse yourself to go to the restroom, ask someone for help, or tell a waiter, the people at the next table—anyone—and just get out. If you are concerned about physical danger, call the police and make sure there are others nearby while you wait for help to arrive.

- **Don't be a fool in love.** Even when you feel you have met the "right" person for you, tread carefully and keep your defenses in place. Always make careful choices regarding any information you provide or the level of intimacy you engage in. While this person might truly be the right fit for you, bear in mind that building trust and credibility is also a key predatory tool.

- **Report fakes and other predators.** The best online dating sites dedicate resources to quality control and respond quickly to reports of abuse, but no site can catch everything. Use the systems provided to report members who don't behave appropriately, and if your concerns aren't dealt with satisfactorily, switch sites.

- **If a date asks you for a loan or any financial information, no matter how sad the "hard luck" story, it is virtually always a scam and you should report it.** If their stories weren't convincing, con artists would never make money. Remember that scam artists are pros at manipulation of your pocket book, your information, and sadly, sometimes your heart.

CHAPTER TWELVE

Step 9: Don't Browse Indiscriminately

"I am writing to tell you how disappointed I am with your Internet service,"
wrote Pamela to her ISP company, still fuming over the incident her son Matt
had experienced the night before.

"We switched to your service recently, and my husband set up parental con-
trols with content filtering to stop access to or search results that include Web
sites we don't approve of. We are very careful to protect our three children.

"Imagine our horror when our 12-year-old son, while searching for informa-
tion on skin diseases for a school project, was inundated with pornographic
images. He tried to close them, but they kept appearing faster than he could
shut them down. He was very, very upset by the experience, and so am I.

"My husband took a look at our settings again and realized he had
neglected to click a final button that enables the changes, so our children were
left completely vulnerable. Apparently your service sets access to filth as the
default, rather than providing even minimal protections for new and existing
members.

"Why aren't you protecting us? Do you think most people appreciate having
pornography thrown at them or at their children? How can a company that
claims to make products for families default their settings to the basest tastes
for content? You should default to the highest family values and allow people
to opt in to filth rather than shove it at the rest of us. If this is how you support
family values, we will be inclined to opt out of the Internet entirely."

Pamela finished the letter, signed her name, and put it in an envelope. But the damage to her son had been done.

What Just Happened?

Pamela's outrage is clearly evident in the letter to her ISP, and she is not alone. In fact, according to research conducted for Consumer Reports WebWatch in 2005, nearly all adult Internet users feel that the ease with which you can stumble across sexually explicit material is a problem; 82 percent feel that it is a *major* problem. Further, 86 percent of all adults online believe there should be a Web site rating system similar to those used for movies and video games. What might surprise you more is that this attitude is also shared by teens and younger children.

About 25 percent of young people who use the Internet are exposed to unsolicited sexual material in a year, although that number might be deceptively low because most don't tell. Their silence reflects not only their shock and embarrassment but also a concern that they might be blamed for doing something wrong if they come forward (Finkelhor et al., 2000).

Matt is an exception in that he talked to his parents about what happened. Only 39 percent of teens tell their parents when they encounter pornography online, and in 44 percent of incidents, the teens tell no one at all (Finkelhor et al., 2000).

Find Out More

See Chapter 17, "Talking About Safety," for advice about creating an environment where it is safe for your child to tell you when a problem occurs.

Although Pamela was frustrated with her service provider, most reputable companies work hard to improve protections and provide settings that enable users to manage their online experience in accordance with their own lifestyles and values. Still, people make many assumptions about the default protections that software companies or Internet service providers have put in place, as Pamela and her family found out the hard way.

In reality, many companies do not test their software for safety at all. They develop cool features and then make them available without providing adequate instructions for their safe use. Sometimes a software company's rush to beat a competitor to market with new features takes precedence over providing products that have been tested for safety.

What Are Parental Controls?

Parental controls is a term for software tools that help parents manage their children's online experiences. Parental control services often include the following features:

- **Content filters** enable you to block access to Web sites that have certain kinds of content.

- **Communication filters** manage which communication tools (such as e-mail or instant messaging) your children are permitted to use and with whom they can communicate.

- **Computer security settings** block some or all applications or file types from being downloaded onto a computer.

- **Access settings** set limits to the amount of time your child can spend online.

- **Reporting tools** provide periodic reports to you about your children's activities online.

Some products contain additional tools that enable you to further monitor someone's activities by detailing every keystroke they make, showing snapshots of what they see on the screen, or even allowing you to read every e-mail or instant message they send or receive.

Pet Peeve

Frankly, parental controls is a term I don't care for. According to global research conducted by Information Solutions Group on behalf of Microsoft, at least 60 percent of parents worldwide don't appreciate this phrase either. Most of you don't want to "control" your children; you want to provide a safer environment so you and your family can enjoy a rich, positive experience on the Internet that matches your family's values and preferences. The term not only offends and potentially deters these people from adopting the technology, it also creates the misperception that the only people who want or need a safer experience are children. Unfortunately, the term parental controls is still the main industry catch-all phrase for these kinds of safety settings and protections in general.

Consumers of all ages naïvely believe that software and online services are safe because they assume software companies spend a great deal of time anticipating how people might abuse their products. Just as you can't assume that your school is spending significant time instructing your children on how to use the Internet safely, it is unrealistic to assume that software manufacturers could possibly account for every vagary of human behavior when producing software features. You are still the best first line of defense when using technology products and services.

Assessing the Risks

Searching and browsing is how we all navigate online, and, as evidenced by research by the Pew Internet & American Life Project shown in Table 12-1, it has become a critically important way for us to get the information we need.

Table 12-1 The Growing Role of the Internet in Decision-Making

Number of Americans for whom the Internet was crucial or important at major moments (*in millions*)		
Activity	2005	2002
Gotten additional training for your career	21	14
Helped another person with a major illness or medical condition	17	11
Chosen a school or college for yourself or your child	17	12
Bought a car	16	13
Made a major investment or financial decision	16	11
Found a new place to live	10	7
Changed jobs	8	7
Dealt on your own with a major illness or other health condition	7	5

Sources: Pew Internet & American Life Project March 2005 survey. N=1,450 for Internet users. The January 2002 survey contained 1,415 Internet users. The margin of error is ±3% for the sample of Internet users in both surveys.

However, there are millions of Web sites online. While a large percentage of these sites might be excellent resources, there is no universal quality assurance guarantee. You must rely on your trust of the Web site owner and the strength of your technology tools (content filters; anti-phishing, antivirus, and anti-spyware programs; pop-up blockers; and so on) for your safety. (Refer to the "Technology Toolkit" section in Part Four for more information on available tools.)

Usually, when we browse, we end up at the site we intended to go to, see the content we expect, and interact with legitimate businesses and well-intentioned people. However, the hazard of browsing is that you or your child might land on a site that has inappropriate content, be redirected to an inappropriate site, or provide personal information on a site that will misuse it. It is also possible that you will unknowingly download spyware, malware, or computer viruses while browsing a less reputable site.

Taking a Closer Look at the World of Online Pornography

Teens (ages 12 to 17) view more Internet pornography than any other segment of the population, but just because your child was directed to a pornographic site does not mean they were searching for pornography or that they viewed it intentionally. Data suggests that 90 percent of kids between 8 and 16 have seen pornography while browsing, but many say they were working on homework at the time. Table 12-2 gives an overview of how often children are exposed to pornography online (adapted from Family Safe Media: www.familysafemedia. com/pornography_statistics.html).

Table 12-2 Children's Exposure to Pornography

Exposure	Age/Percentage
Average age of first Internet exposure to pornography	11 years old
Largest consumer of Internet pornography	12 to 17 age group
15- to 17-year-olds having multiple hard-core exposures	80%
8- to 16-year-olds having viewed porn online	90% (most while doing homework)
Youths who receive sexual solicitations on social networking sites like chat rooms	89%
Youths who receive sexual solicitations in a year	20%

What kind of browsing practices can have these results? In a survey of kids and online pornography conducted by Family Safe Media (www.familysafemedia.com), kids encountered offensive images most often

- While surfing (47 percent)
- When they had misspelled Web addresses (17 percent)
- When they clicked on a link in a Web site (17 percent)

Consider that there are estimated to be 4.2 million pornographic Web sites out there, and they all want you to visit them. In fact, some pornographers actually use children's favorite cartoon character names on their sites specifically so that children will find their sites in online searches.

Adults are no less at risk for seeing content they find undesirable, though they are usually less shocked and distressed by what they see or read. Given their life experiences, adults are more likely than children to simply ignore inappropriate content and move on.

Find Out More

Landing on sites that contain inappropriate material isn't the only browsing hazard. Both adults and children are often tricked into believing they are on a legitimate site and enter information that leaves them open to identity theft attacks. See Chapter 14, "Step 11: Get Savvy About Financial Scams and Fraud," for more information about Web sites that are designed to deceive.

Protecting Yourself

The Web is much like your own town, where there are good parts of town and bad parts of town. You need to be sure you are comfortable with the section of town you choose to spend time in. Unfortunately, it is harder to judge the quality of an Internet neighborhood because it's easier to make a seedy site look like a posh neighborhood.

Consider Your Safety Zone

First, consider the level of safety you feel is important for yourself and your family. Understand the potential pitfalls when surfing and interacting with sites, and how to avoid the parts of the Internet you prefer not to encounter. Teach your children the same skills. Then find the tools to help you avoid access to certain types of sites and content.

Avoid Phony or Dangerous Sites

Identifying which sites are safe and which pose risks, such as delivering spyware or malware to your computer, can be difficult. The people who are proliferating spyware are very good at their jobs. They spend a lot of time figuring out what scam might lure you into downloading their files, as well as searching for new technologies to help them achieve their goals.

Although you certainly can't spend your days keeping up with the latest scams, you can follow a few simple guidelines:

- Don't be fooled into trusting a site because you see reputable advertising there. Just because a well-known company has placed advertising on a site does not mean they endorse the site. It might also be that their brand logo has been hijacked and put there by con artists in an attempt to make the site appear legitimate.

- Use a browser such as the latest version of Internet Explorer or one that provides an alert if you land on a suspicious site, or use a program such as SiteAdvisor that displays alerts as to the risk for encountering spyware or malware delivery.

- Use a free spyware detection program such as Windows Defender, AVG Anti-Virus Free Edition, HijackThis, or Lavasoft Ad-Aware SE Personal Edition on a regular basis to scan for spyware. While these programs cannot catch everything, they will catch most spyware and adware. If you have never run a spyware detection program, do so now, and see what's currently on your computer. You might be surprised.

Think About It

Free spyware detection products usually put the responsibility on you to scan your personal computer frequently to check for spyware. You might prefer to use a for-pay product, such as Windows Live OneCare or Lavasoft's Ad-Aware SE Plus, that you can set up to automatically scan, block, and remove any programs identified as potentially invasive or harmful.

- Links in e-mail, in instant messages, and on Web sites will sometimes appear to lead you to a legitimate site, but that's not always where you end up. When you click any link, double-check the URL displayed in your browser for that site to make sure you landed where you thought you would—especially if you are going to provide passwords or personal information, or bank or shop. See Chapter 14 for more information about financial scams.

Take Advantage of Technology

Learn about and use browser settings and software products to help you gain control of your browsing results:

- Set your browser protections to a level that matches your browsing comfort level. These settings help control whether certain images will be displayed but cannot fully substitute for robust content filtering products. Figure 12-1 shows how you can choose from various Internet security levels.

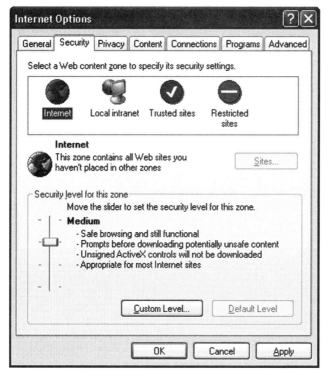

Figure 12-1 The Internet Options dialog box can be reached from Control Panel in Microsoft Windows XP.

- Use pop-up blockers that are built into your browser or through popular downloadable search toolbars from established companies. If spyware gets onto your system, it can cause pop-ups to appear that might contain inappropriate content. A good pop-up blocker will allow you to specify that pop-ups are allowed on trusted sites, enabling you to shop or access entertainment or research on safe sites, and avoid pop-ups on suspect sites.

- Consider all the devices you and your family might use to browse the Internet. Check to see what browsing safeguards are used by your child's school, the local library, and even the families of your child's closest friends to be sure you are comfortable with their protections. Find out what protections your workplace provides. Ask your mobile carrier what kinds of content filtering and browser settings they have available for any Internet browsing done through your family's mobile phones. If you aren't happy with the answers you receive, let the provider know it. Talk to the school district, the library, your cellular provider, your employer, or the parents of your child's friends, and let them know what you expect.

Find Out More

"Technology Toolkit" in Part Four discusses in more detail specific tools and controls you can use to protect yourself and your family.

If a Web site is owned by a reputable company and has clear privacy policies that you have reviewed and are comfortable with, you should feel reasonably safe in browsing there. It is when you are simply surfing around—even with the best tools currently available—that you might potentially increase your exposure to many types of criminal activities.

Be Alert as You Browse

Here are some examples of the tactics some sites employ to trick you.

Let's say you go to a gaming site that claims its service is free. You are asked to enter your name and click a button labeled "I agree to the site terms" (see Figure 12-2 on the next page for an example of site terms). Oops! Did you read those terms? They included giving the site permission to use and sell your personal information to drive direct marketing to you. The other way the site earns money is to reserve the right to redirect you to other Web sites that pay them through banner ads, pop-ups, and other methods (such as e-mail and IM). You cannot hold the company liable for any of that content, advertising, or for any damage or losses you might incur from accessing those other sites.

As you browse, you might also encounter sites that seem safe but that serve up offensive ads. You might, for example, find it inappropriate that your child be exposed to ads for "intimate relationships." Also be aware that some ads that try to get kids or adults to click on them are distribution methods for a fair amount of spyware, adware, or other forms of malware.

Terms of Use for Contoso Games   **ContosoGames**

Information you submit to Contoso Games is your property, but *by submitting the information you grant Contoso the right to use the information for marketing purposes. Including, but not limited to, sharing this information with 3rd parties, direct marketing offers to you including via e-mail, telemarketing, direct mail and text messaging.*

1. When you enter your registration data, you commit to providing accurate, complete information. You guarantee that we can rely on your data to be accurate and complete. *You agree to update your registration whenever a change is made to keep it accurate and complete.*

2. You must agree to abide by all our terms and conditions. *This agreement is subject to change at any time and changes will be posted on this website. It is your responsibility to refer to this page to understand changes or amendments to the original agreement.* If you do not agree with all the terms and conditions in their entirety, you are not authorized to use this website or service in any way.

3. *This website may provide hyperlinks, advertisements, pop-ups or other online methods to redirect you to third party sites* and resources. Because Contoso Games has no control over such sites, *you agree that Contoso is not responsible or liable for any content, advertising or services or for any damages and or losses you may incur therefrom.*

Figure 12-2 Be careful of fine print when browsing.

One particularly obnoxious trick some sites use is to automatically download a different search toolbar that replaces your existing search engine with the one they are being paid to promote. There won't be any message asking for your permission; the switch will just "happen." It will be your job to figure out how to restore your preferred browser.

Taking Charge of Your Browsing Experience

You should never assume that tools alone will keep you or your child safe. No tools can replace common sense and solid, interactive parenting. Companies who build safety tools can promise only that they will try to keep people safe who want to be safe, make it relatively cumbersome to circumvent the safety settings, and warn those who are placing themselves at risk that they are at risk. Learning to browse intelligently, and teaching your family to browse intelligently on reputable sites, gives you important weapons in your online safety arsenal.

Consider the analogy to crossing the road: You can teach a child to look both ways. You can even put up a barrier rail between the sidewalk and the road. But if a child is determined to run across without looking, they'll jump the rail and take off. A child doesn't have to be a computer genius to "hack" the computer or dodge the service's safety barriers. No doubt someone has posted those tricks online. Sometimes a predator tells them how to do it.

Create a framework of education and communication that teaches your family about the risks, and use appropriate tools and settings to create a safer online environment for you and your family.

CHAPTER THIRTEEN

Step 10: Use Common Sense When Gaming with Others

Kaylyn logged in to the gaming site her big brother had shown her the night before. The site was aimed at younger kids, and 10-year-old Kaylyn had enjoyed creating her player identity last night with her brother watching. The pictures of the characters were cute, and she got to pick her own player name. She chose CuteKitten because she loves cats.

After logging in, she clicked on a game to join. There was another person already playing, and she quickly got caught up with the game's action. At one point the other player said over the headset, "Hey, CuteKitten, how old are you?"

"I'm 10," she replied, her attention still on the game.

Then he said that he wanted to send her an instant message. She rattled off her IM name, still trying to keep up with the game. Her young female voice came over loud and clear through the in-game voice system.

A moment later her IM window popped open with the message, "Where do you live?"

"Outside Detroit," Kaylyn replied. "It's a town called Somerset. You probably never heard of it."

Back in the game, Kaylyn was hit, but not fatally, so she quickly got moving again.

"What school do you go to? Maybe you should just give me your phone number and we can talk for real after the game. It's hard talking and playing at the same time, don't you think?"

Just then Kaylyn's mother came in to tell her that her friend Cindy was on the phone. With a sigh, Kaylyn typed, "Gotta go. 'Bye." and logged out of the game site. Her mother wondered what she had been doing. She would remember to ask her when Kaylyn got off the phone.

What Just Happened?

Gaming sites are another place online where you can encounter a variety of people. They can be great places to socialize, to learn strategy skills, and develop creativity. They also provide a channel for meeting and interacting with folks like you who like to make new friends online.

However, it's important to remember that players often have fictional identities as part of the game so you don't know who they really are. They might also be able to chat with you during the game, and harassment or attempts to get personal information do occur. To help avoid exposure to interactions that might be harmful, talk with your kids about safety if they are gamers and about using safety features, and if you are a gamer, educate yourself about any risks.

Kaylyn's brother hadn't taught her any safety rules about **gaming** online. He felt she was on a safe site because it was geared toward younger children and had cute cartoon player characters rather than threatening warrior figures. Her brother had introduced her to the game, so Kaylyn never even thought about any need for safety, and talking to people in the game didn't feel at all like breaking the family rule about not talking to strangers. It was all just pretend. The gamer handle she chose, though seemingly innocent to a 10-year-old, suggested her gender and age.

Because they bought the **game console** for Kaylyn's very responsible older brother, they hadn't even thought about setting up protections they would have wanted for their 10-year-old daughter. If they had, they could have made certain family settings that

- Managed who could access the console for online gaming
- Set restrictions around who their daughter could play and talk with
- Specified what types of games would be appropriate
- Restricted access to Kaylyn's gaming profile so it's not publicly available

Kaylyn was lucky that her mother had interrupted her before she shared her phone number. A 10-year-old girl is not necessarily a good judge of strangers' motives.

What Is Interactive Gaming?

In the past, computer users played games all by themselves. It was possible to have two players sit side by side and play with two joysticks, or to talk to another gamer on the phone while playing separate games.

Today's **interactive gaming** technology has changed the face of computer games. Multiple play-ers can play a game simultane-ously in real time from anywhere around the world. Interactive games often have features such as voice chat so players can talk to each other while playing. You can participate in interactive games from your computer or use a game console, such as Xbox or Sony PlayStation.

Assessing the Risks

According to Deborah Aho Williamson's research in 2005, 45 percent of American households contain some kind of video game system, and a good portion of those have Internet connections. You can play interactive games from your home computer, and games are even available on some cell phones.

As kids become teens and are left alone in the house more often, they might spend hours playing games, and parents need to know how to regulate which games they play and how they behave in those gaming situations.

Interactive gaming can carry these risks:

- Harassment through text messages or voice chat

- Contact with predators

- Exposure to inappropriate game content, including violence and sexual content

- Addiction—adults and children can become addicted to online games and gambling

Although gaming sites contain many serious gamers who don't want to waste their time chatting or socializing, as interactive game popularity rises, younger and more casual users as well as many more women are joining this culture and using gaming sites as social networking sites.

Think About It

"Can you play next week?"

"No, we're going on vacation."

"Oh, is that a long way from where you live?"

"Only about 25 miles north of here."

"Do you want to call me later?"

"Sure..."

These are typical of the kinds of seemingly casual comments that can help someone locate a gamer. If your child calls, the predator has your child's phone number. *People generally don't teach kids to not call people, they just teach them not to give out their phone number.* That's a mistake—you have to teach both, because with today's technology, by calling somebody else you are handing them your phone number in many cases.

For many children, talking to people while playing a game is just part of the game's fantasy world. This can make it a lot riskier to talk to somebody over a headset in a game setting than to talk to a stranger on the phone because kids are so wrapped up in the game that their focus is not on the conversation. When focusing on the action, children might not stop to consider *what* the "friend" is asking, but just blurt out information without thinking.

Protecting Yourself

The world of online gaming is hugely popular, and with good reason. It offers lots of fun and excitement right from your own home. Many parents prefer having their children at home playing a game to being out on the streets where they know there are dangers. However, it's important to remember that whatever your age, you can be at risk even on the most reputable of sites if you don't know how to play safely.

Steps to Safer Gaming

Follow these steps to safer online gaming:

- When using a console or a Web site, learn how to use the safety features that allow you to limit access to games by maturity level, to restrict user interactions, to block users, or to kick people out of a game if they behave badly. If the necessary safety features are not available, let the game provider know it.

- Report abuse. If the game site doesn't allow you to easily report problems and take action against violators, switch to a different site. You should know that some game services provide more protections and enforcement than others. (Xbox and Xbox Live have great safety settings and abuse reporting tools, for example.)

- Don't share personal information, such as your age, name, gender, phone number, address, and so on, in your profile or in communications with other players.

- Don't give out your friends' or family's personal information.

- Don't set up an offline meeting with somebody you meet in an online game. Never agree to meet in person unless somebody you trust is with you. If you are a child or a teen, talk to your parents first.

- Choose your **user name** or **gamer tag** wisely. Some names suggest your gender or age or attract predators with a sexual connotation. (See Chapter 5, "Step 2: Don't Tell People More Than You Should," for more advice on picking safer names.)

- The gaming industry has clearly defined ratings for games to help guide consumers. These rating systems vary by country, so use the rating information that applies for your location and read the descriptions on the game packaging or Web sites to choose games that are age appropriate. (See "Game Ratings You Should Know.")

- Check out an online preview of games, and check for reviews and recommendations before you buy. Sites such as Xbox Live (*www.xbox.com/en-US/live*), GameSpot (*www.gamespot.com*), GameSpy (*www.gamespy.com*), and IGN (*www.ign.com*) all evaluate games and can help you to select games that are appropriate for you or your children.

- Adjust family settings to limit your child's online interaction with other gamers if you feel they aren't mature enough to communicate safely and to block games that you feel are inappropriate.

- Discuss what your family is comfortable with and then set limits.

Game Ratings You Should Know

Around the world there are various systems for rating the content in games. All of these systems help you make informed choices about which games are appropriate for your family. North America and virtually all of South America use the ESRB (Entertainment Software Rating Board: *www.esrb.org*), which has created a rating system that helps you determine whether a game is appropriate for your children. The ESRB symbols appear on game boxes. They include Early Childhood (EC), which is appropriate for ages 3 and older; Everyone (E) for ages 6 and older; Everyone 10+ (E10+) for ages 10 and older; Teen (T) for ages 13 and older, containing some violence, crude humor, or simulated gambling; Mature (M) for ages 17 and older, containing blood and gore, sexual content, and strong language; and Adults Only (AO) for persons 18 and older, with scenes of intense violence or graphic sexuality. In addition, descriptions of the games should appear on the back of a game box, with even more specific information about language, violence, nudity, blood, alcohol references, and so on.

Find Out More

For a guide to using ESRB ratings, go to *www.microsoft.com/windowsxp/using/ games/getstarted/esrbratings.mspx*.

Outside the Americas, rating systems are considerably more varied. Check on the Web to understand the specific categories and age ranges that are used in your country. For example

- Much of Europe uses the PEGI (Pan European Game Information) system, although Finland and Portugal use variations.

- The United Kingdom and Ireland use PEGI/BBFC (British Board of Film Classification).

- Australia goes by the OFLC-AU (Office of Film and Literature Classification) system, and New Zealand uses OFLC-NZ.

- Japan is guided by CERO (Computer Entertainment Rating Organization).

- Korea uses KMRB (Korea Media Rating Board).

At this time, much of the rest of Asia is lacking a standardized rating system.

CHAPTER FOURTEEN

Step 11: Get Savvy About Financial Scams and Fraud

Arthur went into the den after his morning coffee and turned on his computer. Ever since Evelyn died, he has stuck to familiar routines: checking his e-mail after breakfast to see if the grandkids had sent anything, doing a little gardening before the sun got too strong, going for a walk around the block.

This morning there were just two messages: one from his granddaughter Sophie telling him about her school play; the other from his bank telling him he needed to change his online banking password. Why, he wondered, was the bank always making him change his password? He'd talk to Greg, the bank manager, about it next time he went in.

Arthur clicked the link and, on the Web page that opened, entered his account number for verification, his old password, and then his new password, twice. After clicking the Submit button, he opened Sophie's e-mail. There was a photo of her in her costume for the play. He wished Evelyn could see how ador-able Sophie looked. He clicked Reply and started typing a message.

What Just Happened?

Because Arthur uses online banking, which occasionally asks him to change passwords when accessing his account, he was annoyed but not alarmed when an e-mail message asked him to change his password again. Without thinking, he gave a fraudulent site his bank account number and online password, enabling a criminal to transfer funds out of Arthur's account and into his own.

Find Out More

Chapter 10, "Step 7: Understand Risks of Fraudulent Communications and Protect Yourself," discusses safety issues you should be aware of when using your e-mail account.

What Is Phishing?

Phishing (pronounced "fishing") is one form of online scam that often begins with an e-mail, instant messaging, or a pop-up message. These are often very convincing faked messages that look as though they were sent from a legitimate organization such as your bank, utility company, or a retail business. These messages inform you that there is a problem or an opportunity that requires your immediate attention. They ask you to "validate" your identity by providing personal information, such as your social security number, credit card number, password, or bank account information, on a Web site that looks legitimate but is actually a clever fake. Once the criminals have your information, they use it to steal money and/or your identity.

Find Out More

There are a number of great Web sites where you can learn more about phishing and even test your skill at spotting fakes, including *www.mailfrontier.com/forms/msft_iq_test.html*.

Assessing the Risks

Welcome to the brave new world of electronic finance, where there are fantastic opportunities to shop and transact business from wherever you are, whenever it is convenient. But just as carrying a wallet around in the real world puts you at risk for having your money or ID stolen, spending money online and using electronic account access has its own pitfalls.

You have probably become immune to paper junk mail that touts get-rich-quick schemes or telemarketers who ask you to provide a credit card number to buy something or contribute money to a worthy cause over the phone. You have learned not to respond to these scams or hand over your credit card number to a stranger, and for the most part you probably successfully avoid telephone and print mail attempts to defraud you or steal your money.

Unfortunately, whenever money or personal information is exchanged, criminals lie in wait for an opportunity. Cybercriminals know that many people are still new to online commerce and therefore are less prepared for the types of attacks they might face online. So just as a wily pickpocket in a foreign city counts on your lack of familiarity with the area to make you an easier target, criminals have found opportunity with those who are new to banking and purchasing online. They have adapted old tricks for use in an online environment.

We live in a society where our finances now exist to a great extent in electronic files (whether or not you keep your records online, most banks and online retailers do). Phishing is just one type of financial scam in the online world. Learning what kinds of risks exist will help keep your money safer online.

Think About It

Putting risks in perspective: "Identity theft through the Internet using worms, viruses, spyware, malware, or even phishing may grab the headlines. But these incidents account for less than 10 percent of the total cases of identity fraud" in the United States, according to a survey by Javelin Strategy and Research.

Phishing for Your Money

Phishing scams most often arrive via e-mail, and they convince thousands of victims to enter personal and/or financial information that puts them and their money at risk (see Figure 14-1 on the next page).

While people are becoming more aware of this type of online crime, all too many still fall victim. A study by MailFrontier indicates that about 75 percent of Internet users now consistently spot phishing fraud, a significant increase over the 61 percent noted in a 2004 study. Interestingly, the same study notes that 18- to 24-year-old computer users, who are usually more technically savvy, are *more likely* to be fooled by phishing than older users.

From:	WOODGROVE*BANK* (woodgrovebanks@.con)
Date:	Friday, August 11, 2006 5 PM
To:	Rodney&AnnieZ@email.com
Subject:	Notice: Your account may be compromised

New Financing Offer

We are pleased to offer our best customers this exclusive opportunity to refinance your mortgage rates and *save hundreds of dollars* a month by simply transferring your existing loans into a new low fixed price rate of only 5.75%. Use our instant mortgage rate adjuster to see how much you could be saving every month.

You need to respond quickly – interest rates are rising quickly and these rates won't last. We can only guarantee this rate for 3 more days!

Calculate Savings

Click here **to transfer your loan today** – no closing costs, no hassles… just a lower interest rate to save you money.

Notice:

This message was delivered to you as a service by WOODGROVE*BANK*. We are committed to providing our customers with the best services available. WOODGROVE*BANK* ensures your privacy and preferences. To view our privacy policies click here.

If at any time you wish to stop receiving service notices from WOODGROVE*BANK* please click here.

Please do not forward or reply to this message, it is generated from our automated system. Should you wish to reply to this email please contact our customer service representatives through email here, or call 555-1212 during regular banking hours.

WOODGROVE*BANK* USA 1321 Bank St. Carlsbad New Mexico 62909

Copyright 2001 © WOODGROVEBANK All Rights Reserved.

Figure 14-1 Phishing e-mail uses many tactics. This one requires your account information in order to calculate potential loan refinancing savings.

A recent report from MessageLabs states that "vishing" (**V**oIP+ph**ishing**) is one of the cybercriminal's latest scams. Vishing scams make use of an automated voice message that warns the potential victim of possible fraudulent charges on his or her credit card. When the victim calls the provided toll-free number, he is prompted to enter his credit card informa-tion, which the "vishers" then use to make fraudulent charges. It's impor-tant to note that vishers are able to manipulate the caller ID so that the call appears to be coming from a legitimate bank.

Think About It

Scams vary. It might not be the standard "validate your account" message that fools you. Scams are modified as more people catch on to existing schemes. Remember: Human predators target the weaknesses of human nature.

Asking for Your Money

Some online scams ask you to hand over your money for an investment scheme or as a contribution to a charity. Here's how these work.

Investment fraud lures you with large profits and insider information guaranteed to help you get rich quick. This kind of scam has been around for years and can turn up online or offline. Online investment newsletters

Allen County Public Library

Barcode: 31833050793790
Title: Look both ways : help protect ...
Type: BOOK
Due date: 11/20/2012,23:59

Total items checked out: 1

Telephone Renewal: 421-1240
Website Renewal: www.acpl.info

that offer bogus research, bulletin board posting threads that build up the reputation of a stock to create an investing frenzy, and e-mail scams that spread false information about an investment opportunity have added a virtual twist to old cons.

Charity fraud occurs when you are solicited to contribute to a charity or cause, only to find later that the charity is nonexistent. The people who run these scam Web sites count on your generosity, especially right after a disaster, when you feel a sense of urgency about helping people in need (see Figure 14-2).

Figure 14-2 Disasters bring charity fraud perpetrators out of the woodwork. Creating a fake site like the one shown takes very little time.

Scam sites often have names or URLs similar to established nonprofit organizations and sometimes they even "trick" search engines into placing their site near the top of the results displayed when you perform a search. Another ploy scam artists use is to assume that a good percentage of people will misspell a term such as "tsunami." The scam artists link their sites to search results generated by the misspelled words so that the first charities to appear are fraudulent.

Just as you always have, research charities that you aren't familiar with before handing over your money. Many phishing scams today are so convincing that even a trained eye might have a hard time spotting them. That's why, in addition to using a careful eye, it's important to take advantage of anti-phishing technology.

Stealing Your Identity

Attachments to online messages, including e-mail, instant messages, or files posted to sites, can contain malicious software. When you open an attached file, this "malware" is then downloaded to your computer without your knowledge. Such an attachment might contain one or a number of malicious programs designed to harm you or your computer. One type of program that is frequently used to steal identities is called spyware. Some types of spyware allow your online activities to be tracked—including entry of online passwords, personal information, and account numbers—without you being any the wiser, unless you have spyware detection tools installed.

Or, a thief might invite you to become a member of his Web site, asking you to enter your personal information, including a credit card number, to complete the process. He might even provide a real service or product, such as a downloadable game, so that you are more likely to provide the information and are not able to determine how your identity or banking information was stolen.

Once a criminal obtains your personal information, he or she can use it to apply for credit cards in your name, withdraw money from your accounts, charge merchandise online, and more effectively assume your identity. Because kids are more inclined to click on ads, open e-mail and attachments, or take surveys, children's sites are some of the worst offenders for feeding spyware and other malware onto your computer. It is important to teach your children not to click on ads, pop-ups, and links unless they are sure the ad is legitimate and the link comes from a reputable source.

Think About It

When you check your credit history, you should also check the credit history of your children (which is free) to be sure their identities haven't been stolen. Identity scams can saddle your kids with a bad credit history before they even get their first job.

Going Once, Going Twice . . .

When you buy or sell something through an online auction site, you are often not transacting business with a brick-and-mortar company, but with another individual or a virtual company. The basic protections many physical businesses provide aren't available in this scenario. For example, a seller on an auction site might take your money and never deliver the goods or deliver merchandise that is not what you thought it would be. When you try to return faulty merchandise, the seller has disappeared. Again, make sure you do your research. There are legitimate auction sites that provide many of the basic protections you would find in a brick-and-mortar store.

How to Spot Financial Scams

Well-executed scams are hard to spot, even for experts, so always use caution—and follow a few guidelines. Always be suspicious if

- An e-mail message asks you to update or enter personal information and provides a link.

- There's a sense of urgency, such as a limited-time offer. Cyber-criminals hope you'll be so eager to act, that you won't stop to think.

- The e-mail or Web site contains grammatical errors or misspellings. Reputable companies rarely have such errors. However, keep in mind that as criminals get more sophisticated their spam and phishing scams have matured, and many will no longer make "amateur" spelling mistakes.

- The Web site's URL is subtly different than the actual company name. Remember that some domain names are registered with common misspellings for a URL so that you might land on their site by mistake and proceed to do business with them.

Advertising Fraud

Classified ad sites are another area where you're not dealing with a company but with individuals trying to sell your something, just as on an auction site. Most of the warnings about online auctions that you'll read in the next section pertain to classified ad sites, as well.

Scams involving advertising can include online classified ads for products or services that are fraudulent or misrepresentative. Reputable classified sites such as Windows Live Expo (*http://expo.live.com*) and craigslist (*www.craigslist.org*) post advice about how to use their services and warnings to help you avoid getting stung, and they monitor their sites for abuse.

> **Think About It**
>
> Shopping online is not only convenient, it can often save you money, and it can be as safe as shopping in a store or by mail as long as you follow some basic guidelines. An excellent resource for safer Internet shopping is the U.S. government site *http://onguardonline.gov/shopping.html*. These recommendations apply to users worldwide.

Protecting Yourself

Depending on the type of financial scam you encounter, there are several things you can do to protect yourself.

Don't Hand over Your Cash

You probably wouldn't invest your hard-earned money in an investment scheme touted by a total stranger in a phone call. So why would you invest in response to an e-mail from a total stranger? One problem with e-mail scams is that they can look so professional and link you to an entire Web site that looks very official. This convinces the unwary that they are doing business with a reputable company when, in fact, there might be only a solitary scam artist behind the whole thing. But when you learn to see through the online bells and whistles, avoiding online financial scams is simply a matter of applying the same caution to the Internet that you use in your everyday offline financial dealings.

There are two great rules of thumb to follow to avoid online schemes that separate you from your money:

- If it sounds too good to be true, it probably is. When you see a message or pop-up telling you that you can make $75,000 by investing $5, or that you can get rich quick if you click this link in the next minute, or that you have won a sweepstakes but must send $23.97 for shipping and handling and fill in your personal information to receive the prize, then run, don't walk, away. And always report such e-mail to your service provider. This helps them block future messages or pop-ups of this type.

- No reputable company or organization will ask you to enter your account number, social security number, password, or other information via e-mail or pop-up. Avoid using links to a site from an e-mail message that is asking you for information. If you do decide to go to the site, look it up in a search engine or type in the URL yourself. If you go to the site yourself and note that it is a secure site (many sites "look" like they are secure to fool you, so be sure it's also a company you trust), entering information in forms is fine, but if you haven't initiated the contact, don't provide information.

Here is the U.S. Securities and Exchange Commission's advice about spotting and avoiding online investment scams:

- Get the facts. Never, ever make an investment based solely on what you read in an online newsletter or bulletin board posting, especially if it involves a small, thinly traded company that isn't well known.

- Get financial statements from the company and analyze them.

- Verify claims about any new product developments or lucrative contracts.

- Avoid offshore investment opportunities. If you send your money abroad and something goes wrong, it's difficult to find out what happened and to locate your money.

- Check out the people running the company and find out if they've ever made money for investors before.

> ### Find Out More
> For a detailed list of questions you should ask before investing, visit *www.sec.gov/investor/pubs/askquestions.htm*.

Auction Safely

Auctions can be a great way to find a deal, but not when the deal turns out to be a phony. When using an online auction site, follow these guidelines:

- Use only reputable sites and carefully read the safe buying and selling tips they provide. Good sites update their safety tips as new scams appear and will try to warn you of what you should be on guard against.

- If the site displays a rating of a user's reputation taken from buyer or seller comments about their shopping experience, check out what is being said about the person or company. Ask for and confirm a seller's phone number in case you have questions or problems, and save any e-mail correspondence.

- Be very careful about the method of payment you use, and learn what your options are if something goes wrong. If you send a seller a personal check, you might find that the person makes use of your address and bank account information to commit fraud.

- Sellers also get bitten: They run into buyers who take delivery of the product only to find out that the check or credit card information is bad. Often people feel very safe if they are told they will receive a "bank check" or that the money is being wired, but these offers are almost always fraudulent. You might want to use an online transaction company such as PayPal, or use your credit card, which provides you some protection under the Fair Credit Billing Act. Also, when you use a credit card, be aware that you can dispute the charges.

- If the seller offers you a lower price if you will deal with them outside the auction site, walk away. It is most likely a scam. They'll get the money, and you won't ever see the goods.

- Be very clear about what you are bidding on, take care to get a full description of the product, and review any fine print. The most common types of auction fraud by sellers are: failure to send the items purchased; the item purchased has been swapped with an inferior product; failure to ship in a timely manner; or failure to disclose relevant information.

Find Out More

You can learn more about safety precautions you can take with Internet auctions at *http://onguardonline.gov/auctions.html.*

Using Classified Ads Wisely

When you post your e-mail or other contact information in an online ad, you are giving away a valuable commodity to others online who might harass you, try to sell you things, or sell your information to others. If possible, use an e-mail address provided by the listing service, or get a separate e-mail address to use for the duration of the ad. Be careful not to reveal more information than necessary through photos or text, or by providing contact information.

Follow all the advice I just gave you on auction sites when buying and selling via classifieds. Also, read classified sites' safety material. Classified sites recommend that you purchase items only from individuals within your local area so you have better control over the transaction, to be careful of fraudulent payment forms (especially wire transfers), and to report any abuse to the providers of the system.

Understand that no auction or classified site can be responsible if *you* chose to hand over your money or sell your product, and got swindled. They can't get your money back for you, although they will point you to government sites where you can report the crime. Do your research: In any financial transaction, follow the age-old advice of buyer/seller beware.

Think About It

Any international transactions should be researched thoroughly, and if you decide to proceed, do so with extra caution.

Final Words of Advice

The Federal Trade Commission offers several tips to help you to avoid phishing and other financial online scams (and I've added a bit of advice of my own in italics):

- If you get an unsolicited e-mail or pop-up message that asks for personal or financial information, do not reply. And don't click the link in the message, either. *Notify your service provider through their junk mail reporting system (see Figure 14-3).*

Figure 14-3 Your service provider should offer easy ways to report junk mail and scams. With Windows Live Mail (formerly called MSN Hotmail), you see the Report & Delete link at the top of every e-mail message.

- Use antivirus software and a firewall, and keep them up to date. *Also install an anti-spyware program (either use free software and run it frequently, or pay for a program you can set up to automatically run and update) to detect and remove any other malware. You should have automatic updates for your operating system turned on as well so that you receive fixes to any problems that have been exploited by a cybercriminal.*

- Don't send personal or financial information because e-mail is not secure. *This is also true for instant messaging. An exception to this would be encrypted e-mail or IM. If you pay for a service, the odds are that your communications are encrypted; if it's free, verify whether the service uses encryption.*

- Look for indicators that a site where you submit personal information is secure in the form of a lock symbol on the status bar 🔒 or a URL starting with https https://ww. *This isn't foolproof,* as these can be spoofed. However, when used in tandem with other precautions that you take to ensure that you are dealing with a reputable organization, these are helpful.

- Double-check a site before doing business by typing the address into your browser. If you went to a site by clicking a link in, for example, an e-mail message, you might have been redirected and are doing business with a stranger.

- Review credit card and bank account statements as soon as you receive them to check for unauthorized charges. If you have become a victim of identity theft, report it by going to *www.consumer.gov/ idtheft/con_file.htm.*

- Be cautious about opening any attachments or downloading any files from e-mail you receive, no matter who sent the message.

- Forward spam that is phishing for information to *uce@ftc.gov* and to the company, bank, or organization that is impersonated in the e-mail. *Forward spam to your service provider, as well.*

- If you believe your identity has been stolen online, file a complaint at *www.ftc.gov*, and then visit the FTC's Identity Theft Web site at *www.consumer.gov/idtheft* for steps you should take.

CHAPTER FIFTEEN

Step 12: Don't Let Your Defenses Down When Using Mobile Devices

Marco lives in New York City with his mom. His dad moved to Miami after his parents' divorce. Many of his friends already had cell phones, and Marco pleaded with his dad to get him one. On the morning of his 11th birthday, his mom gave him her present, a new pair of jeans and a shirt, and then handed him a package from his dad. Inside was the exact cell phone Marco had asked for.

After school Marco activated the phone and studied the manual. The next day he took it to school, showing it off on the bus and in-between classes. It had super-cool features like a digital camera, a Web browser, and instant messaging. He showed his friends how he could download stuff like games, music, and mini-applications.

After school Marco ran into Tony. Tony was an older kid, a high school dropout who worked at the video arcade. A lot of kids thought Tony was cool and tried to impress him. Tony told Marco that he could use his phone to download pornography, and made it seem like a really cool thing to do. Marco wasn't so sure but let Tony play around with his phone for a few minutes. "See," Tony said, holding up the phone. Marco's jaw dropped when he saw a picture of a naked girl staring back at him. Marco felt kind of uneasy, and as soon as he could, he got his phone away from Tony and headed home.

On the bus he desperately tried to figure out how to delete the picture before his mom could see it. What he didn't realize was that Tony had actually downloaded 10 pictures, charging all of them to Marco's cell phone account. Tony had also e-mailed the photos to himself. When Marco's mom found the other nine pictures, and saw the cell phone bill, Marco would be in big, big trouble.

What Just Happened?

Marco's bragging gave Tony an opportunity to take advantage of Marco's innocence. Marco was left holding the bag: Besides having to explain to his mother where the pictures came from should she discover them, he will also have to deal with the charges for them on his phone bill.

But the most serious damage is that Marco has been exposed to some potentially very disturbing content and introduced to unsavory use of the Internet through his cell phone. Whether he chooses to download more pornography or not, his worldview has changed. He won't forget his exposure to all that's out there, and how easy it is to access via his cell phone.

Cell phones and other mobile devices provide a lot of freedom. They enable people to keep in touch with family and friends while on the road, get work done, send images and files across long distances, and have fun buying content such as ringtones, games, and background graphics. People are doing very creative things with these devices, including photography, school projects, and learning new skills for future jobs in a knowledge-driven economy.

However, mobile devices also carry some specific risk factors that you should know about. One danger is that kids can use features to download inappropriate material, away from the supervising eyes of their parents. The boundaries of what you feel is appropriate for your family might not extend to their purchases of some types of extreme ringtones and background graphics, or to pornography. Not all downloads have an associated charge that a parent can track on a phone bill. They might be purchased through a premium service, or might just be traded among kids. Pornography can also be sent to a child by a predator who is grooming them.

What Is Mobile Computing?

Mobile computing includes a range of portable devices, from personal digital assistants (PDAs) to cell phones, laptop computers, and portable gaming consoles. Today, most of these connect to the Internet through wireless technology, and many allow you to sign on at public and private wireless access points in airports, libraries, restaurants, and at business sites. Many can also connect directly to other mobile devices using a wireless technology called Bluetooth. Mobile devices can send and receive a variety of media, such as e-mail, real-time text messaging, video, and voice.

Assessing the Risks

Mobile phone usage has skyrocketed in just one generation. Over 30 countries around the world have exceeded 100 percent cell phone penetration, which means that there are more cell phone accounts than there are people in those countries. (The United States lags somewhat at around 65 percent, according to Informa Telecoms & Media.) But *how* people of different ages use their mobile phones varies significantly.

Most people over 40 years of age use their mobile phones because of the convenience of being able to make and receive calls anywhere. Younger users consider their cell phones as portable computers and use them to interact, entertain, inform, and create new content in a wide variety of ways. And users are getting ever younger. In the United Kingdom, two-thirds of children aged 8 to 15 own a mobile phone (49 percent of 8- to 11-year-olds and 82 percent of 12- to 15-year-olds), with the sharpest increase in mobile phone ownership now being between the ages of 10 years old (40 percent of kids) and 11 years old (78 percent of kids) according to research by Ofcom. (Office of Communications is the regulator for the UK communications industries.)

What this means for parents is you might have a learning gap that hampers your ability to help protect your children's mobile safety. If you aren't familiar with all the features of your child's phone, have them show and explain all the cool functions to you.

Mobile device risks fall into several categories, including theft, encouragement of inappropriate behavior because of their portable and personal nature, and ways in which predators can use them to stalk or harass.

The High Rate of Mobile Device Theft

The most likely risk you and your child face is that your mobile device gets stolen. In this situation, the actual loss includes the sense of vulnerability that comes with theft, the value of the device itself, *plus* the value of any information stored on it. This might include the address book (and exposure of everyone in it), calendar information that might include locations and times you'll be away from home, any messages you've stored that can be read, stored personal information, and links to banks with stored passwords. In addition, there is the concern that the thief will try to run up charges on your phone bill, so you should always report theft immediately.

Think About It

Theft is the single biggest concern about mobile devices for parents in England, where this trend has become a huge problem. Mobile phones make up 45 percent of the reported theft on the London Underground, according to British police. Across England, a phone is stolen every 12 seconds, at a cost of more than £390 million ($719 million) a year. (Research by Halifax Home Insurance.)

Human Nature and Mobility

Beyond theft, every hazard discussed in this book regarding the posting of personal information online or becoming too trusting of people you have met only online holds true, whether you're using a desktop computer in your den, a cell phone in the mall, or a laptop in a hotel room. But there are other, special concerns when you go mobile that you have to take into account.

Your children's mobile devices such as cell phones are with them 24 hours a day, 7 days a week. There is little opportunity for parental oversight. In fact, cell phones are like the paper diaries of yesteryear in that kids guard their privacy aggressively. Kids count their cell phones as status symbols. Parents often endure a considerable amount of pestering by their kids asking for the latest, greatest phone. Consider carefully what features you feel will be appropriate for your child, as the phone they are asking for might have features that potentially expose your child to more risk than you are comfortable with. In addition, remember that not all the protections that are available on home computers are available on cell phones at this time.

> ### Find Out More
> Some family phone plans, such as those offered with Disney Mobile phones (*http://disneymobile.go.com*), offer family monitoring and call control features that parents of younger children might want to consider.

Phones are being brought to market that can record lengthy videos. One unfortunate manifestation of this in England has been children video recording themselves dodging trains on railroad tracks, and tragically, some have been killed. The ability to "star" in a video is giving a new twist to the old problem of one-upmanship that inspires kids to gain prestige by acting out in dangerous ways.

Another issue on the rise is bullying via mobile phones (Figure 15-1). Some kids are quite vicious toward others. Their behavior is being driven by their having in their possession a powerful communication tool with the ability to record video and take pictures, and share them easily. This instant access to communication is removing the "cooling down" time they might need to reconsider rash actions, and there is some evidence to suggest that kids are behaving more spontaneously and venting feelings and emotions more readily, with negative consequences. According to a 2005 report by ECPAT International, we're witnessing a rise in kids bullying others through mobile devices in the United Kingdom and elsewhere in the world. As the U.S. cell phone market catches up, we are seeing this trend expand in the United States as well, without clear preventative measures. The ability to harass victims 24/7 is powerful—and devastating. In some cases, this has driven the victims to commit suicide.

Figure 15-1 Bullying is never okay. Make sure your children aren't bullies, and that they can come to you if they are being bullied.

Mobile Phone–Specific Dangers

Mobile phones are by far the most ubiquitous mobile device with more than 2 billion users today—nearly three times as many people have mobile devices as have personal computers. A phone is also the mobile device a young person is most likely to carry. Mobile phones enable a selection of functionality for users, but as with all technology, there are some safety considerations in using these functions. Unfortunately, the most publicized safety message about using cellular phones in the United States, New Zealand, Australia, and other countries is that you shouldn't talk while driving your car. The second most hotly discussed safety topic in many countries is whether or not they are linked to cancer. But there are several other safety aspects you should know about.

Predatory contact on cell phones involves different qualities and consequences than those present through a computer, and parents need to understand a fuller range of issues when considering the unique opportunities these provide:

- Mobile phones are personal devices. There is no big screen in the living room that allows parents to check on their children's activities.

- They provide 24-hour direct access to a user, which provides unique opportunities for harassment, solicitation by telemarketers, and obscene callers.

- Young people send hundreds of billions of text messages, and these usually include the phone number of the sender, which makes contacting them easy. The area code provides useful information a predator can use to discover where you live.

- Text messaging, or **SMS** (Short Message Service), has risks similar to Internet chat rooms. You don't always know the identity of the person you are texting with, and it could be a total stranger who starts a conversation with you. Anyone can be hiding behind that phone number, especially if it was bought with a prepaid phone plan.

- Currently cell phones have little or no content filtering mechanisms, so that surfing the Internet might return results that you do not wish to see or expose your children to. This will be changing, however. Both in the United States and abroad, phone service carriers are beginning to provide content filtering features. Ask your carrier if they offer these services. If your carrier hasn't rolled out content filtering yet, ask when it will be available. Remember that you drive the cellular phone companies' business. If enough parents ask for feature-level filtering options, mobile operators will begin providing these services.

- Most phones sold today have photo and video capabilities that allow you or your children to send or receive images that might or might not be acceptable to you. If your phone is **Multimedia Messaging Service (MMS)** enabled, the photos do not even need to be opened separately. They simply appear when you open the message—and you might be startled by what is sent.

- Your cell phone might be capable of using location services that allow users to let others see where they are. Keep in mind that a key factor in predation is access. Letting people know where you are must be done with deliberate considerations.

Protecting Yourself

Perhaps you've helped to protect your child from online dangers by keeping the computer in an open place in your home where you can occasionally check on things. Now consider for a moment that the mobile phones kids carry today are really small computers—ones that you might have taken no precautions for.

Many cell phones have advanced Internet services available, the ability to communicate with anyone at any time, and are completely private. Because children will be on their own with their cell phones, you have to instill in them an understanding about the potential dangers of communicating with anybody they don't know, broadcasting personal information, opening images or files they receive, swapping copyrighted information, or exposure to inappropriate content.

Guidelines for Safe Mobile Computing

Here are some discussion guidelines and possible rules of the road for you and your children to consider if they are using mobile devices:

- Your child's phone number automatically becomes their instant message address, and this can be easily spammed or used to identify children to predators. Children should never ever communicate with strangers in any way through their phone. They should not answer instant messages, text messages, accept downloads, or send videos. They should never give a phone number to strangers or post a mobile phone number online.

- Protect the phone with a password or PIN so others can't use it without permission.

- Bullying isn't okay. Ever. Explain the consequences if your children engage in it, and ask them to tell you if it happens to them.

- Many parents prefer prepaid phone plans to monthly bills, to set clear spending limits and avoid surprises on their phone bill. One safety consideration in choosing a prepaid plan is whether you can request a monthly statement detailing who called your child, who your child called, and what they might have purchased through their phone. If the carrier cannot provide this overview for a pre-paid plan, you might prefer using a standard billing plan so you can review the bill for potential issues.

- It can be fun to walk around flashing a fancy phone, but as with flashing any prestigious object, this can make a child a target for theft. When they aren't using it, the phone should be kept out of sight. If they wouldn't wave their wallet in public, they shouldn't wave their phone around.

- If a phone gets stolen, report it to your carrier and the police right away. If you haven't already written down the phone's serial number and stored it in a safe place, do it now. Check your manual or ask your provider if your phone is GSM based. If it is, write down both the IMEI (International Mobile Equipment Identity) number that can be found by entering *#06# into the phone or on the label on the back of your battery *and* the serial number. You will need this information when you call the police and your carrier to get your phone service stopped.

- Consider carefully whether tracking technologies are appropri-ate for your family. Remember that there are two kinds of location services: harmless active services that help you locate restaurants, theaters, and so on; and passive services that allow an individual phone to be tracked. Many of these latter types of applications are free of charge, and both kids and adults download them so their friends, and friends of their friends, can see where they are. However, you should consider carefully whether you feel it is appropriate for their online contacts, who might include people they've never met, to be able to track them. Many companies now tout this as a great way for parents to know where their kids are (in itself, this might be overly invasive, depending on their age). However, this is also potentially a great way for predators to know where kids (or you) are, or for an abusive harasser, spouse, or boyfriend to track you (or your child).

Think About It

Tracking technologies only track the phone, not your child. In many cases, it's just as easy to call your children and ask where they are as it is to track them.

Find Out More

Check out the Cellular Telecommunications & Internet Association (CTIA) guidelines at *http://files.ctia.org/pdf/16WirelessContentClassification.pdf*. The CTIA made this statement about the need for these guidelines:

"With the wide variety of content including video, games, music, and ringtones available to wireless subscribers, the cellular industry recognized its responsibility as content distributors to proactively develop the tools and controls consumers need to make informed choices when accessing carrier content. The industry's work culminated in the development of the 'Wireless Content Guidelines'. . ."

• Find out if your kids swap downloaded content with others. Advise them that if the material is copyrighted, it might be illegal for them to do so. If content sent to them is inappropriate, help them understand they should come to you for help in solving the issue. Sharing pornographic content is often an early step in the predatory grooming process of a child, establishing a way to reward children and to introduce steadily more graphic sexual images and normalize sexual behaviors for a child. Report it to your carrier and the police should that be warranted.

• Your kids should be careful about using their mobile device's photo or video technology to send pictures or videos of themselves to anybody they don't know. Even when shared with somebody they know, pictures and videos should not include anything that might embarrass them. Once the picture or video is sent, they will no longer have control over where it goes next. If they aren't comfortable with it being sent around their school or to you, they shouldn't send it (or create it).

- Many children enjoy playing games on their mobile devices. Some of these games are single-player games, and some are hosted online where children can interact with other players. If they are playing interactive multiplayer games, your kids need to know safe chatting rules, and they need to know which games are appropriate for their age.

- Some mobile devices are marketed primarily as gaming consoles. These might have **Subscriber Identity Module (SIM)** cards so they can communicate with other players. Check the features of such a device before you buy it, and consider your choices with your family's needs in mind.

- Children might use their phone as a place to store information or images that they don't want their parents to know about. Some phones can now hold quite a lot of data, and phones that use memory cards can store even more. Sit down with your child to review their content as appropriate. You might choose to simply not purchase a phone that uses memory cards in order to limit the amount of content that can be stored.

- Help kids understand that they need to read the fine print before subscribing to premium-rate services to buy ringtones or games. Kids sometimes buy a ringtone for $2 and unknowingly sign up with a subscription service for $12 a month. Some of these are genuine services but others are scams.

Taking It Step by Step

A graduated approach to mobile device ownership and features is a good idea. If you're going to buy a mobile device for a child under 10, you might want to choose something designed for young children, such as the Firefly, which has limited and controlled capabilities.

When you're satisfied that your children understand the risks, and you are confident that they will turn to you for help if a problem arises, graduate them to the next level of features. At some point you have to let them fly on their own, and this milestone almost always comes before parents feel ready.

Start reviewing data stored on your children's phones early on, so it feels normal and not intrusive. Trying to initiate this when your kids are teens might be difficult if not impossible, because they're likely to feel like you're invading their privacy. Striking a balance isn't easy but it's worth the effort.

Good communication with your child and reassurance that if problems arise they won't automatically have their mobile device taken away will make kids more likely to turn to you for help when things go wrong. It's better to solve the problem and use what's happened as a teachable moment than to just blame the child.

CHAPTER SIXTEEN

Step 13: Act to Avoid Harassment and Bullying

Caroline opened the door of her apartment slowly, looking around the small one-room studio and kitchenette as if she expected to see somebody waiting for her there. As she hurriedly shut and locked the door, her cell phone beeped, indicating that she had a text message. As an emergency medical technician, the 23-year-old had to keep her phone on even when she was off duty, in case she was needed. She hesitantly checked the message.

"Caroline. It's me, Kevin. I know you're home. Shall I come over so we can be together?" the message read.

"Leave me alone!" she screamed at the phone, punching the power button in panic. Kevin had been calling and text messaging her for a week. As she turned on her computer to check her e-mail, she knew there would be messages from him there, as well.

"He keeps coming at me," she had told a friend the night before over a glass of wine. "I don't know if I can stand this much longer. We dated only three times. It's not like I led him on. Why can't he understand I don't want him in my life?"

As she opened her e-mail, a message from Kevin with an attachment appeared in her inbox. He'd never sent an attachment before. She opened it fearfully. It was a photo of her leaving her friend's house the previous night, after having a couple of beers to celebrate her birthday. She had walked home afterward to clear her head. The photo was a little grainy, possibly taken with a cell phone, but she was clearly identifiable. The message said, "Maybe your folks or your boss would like to see what you do in your spare time?"

"Oh no," she moaned. She sat down on her couch, quietly sobbing as she tried desperately to think of a way out.

What Just Happened?

Cyberbullying, cyberharassment, and cyberstalking are all terms for ways in which those who wish to hurt others, for whatever reason, can use online tools to do so. In Caroline's case, the bully is a man she went out with a few times who decided to seek revenge because she rejected him. He used various technologies to get at Caroline, including phone calls, instant messages, text messages, and e-mail.

For Caroline, her harasser was somebody she knew. That is not always the case. Cyberbullies don't have to confront their victims in person or even identify themselves—that's part of the appeal. They can hide in the shadows and threaten. That anonymity can be even more frightening for the victim who doesn't even know who the tormentor is.

What Is Cyberbullying?

Bullying has been around forever, but when you add the tools the Internet provides, bullies can harass victims through a variety of media, 24 hours a day, in private or in very public ways. They can

- Instant message, text message, call, or e-mail insults, accusations, and threats
- Send modified photos of people to their friends and family
- Leave rude and threatening comments on social networking sites
- Create fake blogs, pretending to be the victim to stir up trouble with friends, to entice a predator, to post embarrassing videos, and so on

---

Assessing the Risks

People are becoming comfortable with expressing their feelings online. Sending affectionate e-mail or an online greeting card is a fun way to show you care. Reassuring a distant friend that he or she is valued is a wonderful way to make use of a supportive social network. But as the ways and means of communicating online expand, the opportunity for bullies expands. Just as you can show positive emotions and support for others online, you can show negative and destructive emotions, sometimes in very hurtful and public ways.

"Bullying is as old as the hills, and with young people it's generally linked to stuff at school. Many of us experienced it at some point but when I was a kid, I knew that once I got home and closed the street door behind me, I had a sanctuary. The bullying stayed outside. With new technologies there now is no 'outside' and that can make the bullying even more pernicious and harder to deal with," says John Carr, Chair of the U.K.'s Children's Charities' Coalition on Internet Safety, as well as the New Technology Adviser to NCH (National Children's Home), England's leading children's charity, and an adviser to the European Union's Safer Internet Programme.

Find Out More

The NCH maintains a Web site at *www.stoptextbully.com* that offers excellent advice about dealing with cyberbullying.

Why People Bully Online

Online bullying and harassment is a serious problem around the world. Though the full impact is difficult to measure because of under-reporting, the most recently published research from NCH (2001) indicates that one in four children in the United Kingdom was the victim of online bullying in that year.

The Internet appeals to stalkers and bullies because it offers a certain amount of anonymity. A bully can hide behind temporary e-mail accounts or nicknames in chat rooms or instant messaging programs. When you can hide your identity from your victim or hurl insults from a distance, there is no fear of retaliation. Though the traditional bully might be physically strong, cyberbullies can be physically weak or even younger than their victims, but still cause tremendous psychological pain. Since physical size is no longer required to become an aggressor, and with virtually unlimited access to potential targets, the Internet provides a sort of "equal opportunity offender" environment that allows anyone to act on their feelings.

Harrassment Among Teens: Not So Innocent

In case you think bullying between teens is no big deal, here's a story about how two girls used technology to go after each other.

Shaylyn pulled up Cassandra's blog, and browsed through her entries, trying to find something she could use. She was still furious that Cassie was going to the prom with Daniel, the cutest guy in class. Daniel had dated both girls in recent months, but Shaylyn was sure Cassie had used some trick to get him to ask her to the big dance.

Browsing through Cassie's postings, she noticed one thread where Cassie talked about having gained a few pounds around Christmas. That gave Shaylyn an idea. After downloading a picture Cassie had posted of herself, Shaylyn opened her father's image-editing program. He was a professional photographer and had taught her how to manipulate photos. When she found a photo of an overweight girl, Shaylyn pasted Cassandra's head to it.

With a few more tweaks, she made the photo look plausible. Then she went to Daniel's blog and posted the photo with a note that sounded like it was from Cassandra: "Daniel, I'm really excited to be going to the prom with you. I'll try not to get too chunky between now and then. Love, Cassie."

With a feeling of triumph, Shaylyn posted a picture of herself, wearing tight jeans and a halter top, on her blog with a note about how she had spent her spring break hiking and riding her bike. She then sent an instant message to Daniel and told him to check it out.

Unfortunately, what Shaylyn hadn't anticipated was Cassie's revenge. When Cassie heard about what Shaylyn had done, she created a new blog and posted an altered photo of Shaylyn. Then, pretending to be Shaylyn, Cassie posted a bunch of mean comments about other students and spread the word about the blog.

Think About It

A study of 1,500 Internet-using adolescents in the United States found that over one-third reported being victimized online and over 16 percent admitted to cyberbullying others. Notably, less than 15 percent of victims told an adult about the incident (Hinduja and Patchin, research, fall 2005, currently under peer review).

A Growing Threat

Cyberharassment is growing, and not just among young people. In fact, the prevalence of online bullying has now surpassed traditional bullying offline. Whether such attacks represent a personal vendetta between two adults, the stalking behavior of a complete stranger, or teens ganging up on another teen, these campaigns have at times gone so far that their victims have sought psychiatric treatment or been pushed over the edge to suicide. The schoolyard bully that kids once faced at recess for 20 minutes a day seems tame compared with the online bully who can harass victims through many media 24 hours a day.

Because electronic forums are largely unsupervised, and personal messages are private, those in authority are hard pressed to spot or prevent this harassment. And victims, ashamed of their "weakness," or afraid of further reprisals, are often reluctant to report the abuse. Another problem is the increasingly common presence of computers in the private environments of adolescent bedrooms. Teenagers often know more about computers and cellular phones than their parents and are therefore able to operate these technologies without worrying that a probing parent will discover their experience with bullying (whether as a victim or an offender). In a similar vein, the inseparability of a cellular phone from its owner makes that person a perpetual possible target for victimization.

The Impact of Bullying and Harrassment

Bullying can have serious physical and mental health consequences, which are outlined in Table 16-1. (The information in Tables 16-1 and 16-2 is taken from *www.womedia.org/lgr_statistics_print.htm* and is specific to the United States.)

Table 16-1 The Effects of Bullying

Consequence	Source
An estimated 160,000 children miss school every day out of fear of attack or intimidation by other students.	National Education Association, 1995
One out of every 10 students who drops out of school does so because of repeat bullying.	Oklahoma Health Department, 2001
Those who are bullied are five times more likely to be depressed and far more likely to be suicidal.	Fight Crime: Invest in Kids, September 2003

Bullying takes a tremendous and often long-lasting toll on the lives of the victims and of bystanders (see Table 16-2).

Table 16-2 Bullying Affects the Vast Majority of Youth

The Scope of the Problem	Source
66 percent of youth are teased at least once a month, and nearly one-third of youth are bullied at least once a month.	2002 National Survey of Students Grades 5–12, Families and Work Institute
For children in grades 6 through 10, nearly one in six (or 3.2 million) are victims of bullying each year, and 3.7 million are bullies.	Fight Crime: Invest in Kids, September 2003
Over the course of a year, nearly one-fourth of students across grades reported that they had been harassed or bullied on school property because of their race, ethnicity, gender, religion, sexual orientation, or disability.	2001–2002 California Student Survey

For some parents of bullies, there is a strong tendency to minimize or dismiss the behavior of their child. They consider such behavior as being "just a phase," or say that "kids will be kids." Some consider that kids will just work out confrontations among themselves. Often this viewpoint is accompanied by the attitude that the victim should "toughen up." Not only does this point of view utterly disregard the tremendous damage done to victims, it also fails to recognize the very dangerous path bullies themselves walk. Unchecked bullying can escalate to more serious violence.

Protecting Yourself

You've probably learned to deal with occasional road rage that occurs in rush-hour traffic. Now you must learn to deal with online "road rage" so you can enjoy the benefits of the Internet and avoid or halt its abuses.

Throughout this book, I offer many warnings about carefully considering whether you make your contact information, emotions, or personal photos and videos publicly available online. These considerations are a good starting point for thwarting the random cyberbully. If bullies don't know how to find you, it's harder for them to attack online. If they don't have your photo, they can't manipulate it to embarrass you.

Think About It

Talk to your children about online bullying. Explain to them what it is and how to avoid it, and to talk to you if they receive it. Tell them why they should never bully others, and make clear what the consequences will be for that type of behavior. It's a good idea to keep your home computer out in the open where your children can't easily use it to bully others and you can see if they are receiving harassing messages. Also, talk to them about the messages they might be receiving through their phones or other devices.

The next defense against bullying is to report it. Encourage your children to report bullying to you, and then, if necessary, report it to your Internet service provider or cell phone company. You should expect prompt intervention by your provider. If abuse results from an interaction with a business, such as an online auction or classified ad site, notify that business of the abuse. In many cases, they will ban the harasser from their site or chat rooms. In extreme cases, you can report harassment to the police. Often the FBI and Internet service providers work together to gather evidence and enforce laws in online harassment cases. But they can't do a thing if nobody reports the abuse.

There are many resources that can help you and your children deal with online bullying. Don't suffer in silence; instead, take action. If you or your child becomes a victim, follow these guidelines:

- If you feel that you or your child is in any way unsafe, call the police. Don't hesitate or wait to see if it will stop.

- If you're an adult who is being bullied, harassed, or stalked, report the abuse to your ISP, mobile service provider, and/or any Internet service that is being used to abuse you. Have them take action against the abuser and help you understand how you can block undesirable people from contacting you. If they don't provide you the support you need, change companies and let them know why you changed.

- If you're a parent, talk to your children so they know to come to you if they are bullied, and then take action on their behalf. If these issues are related to school in any way, call the school and report it. They should have strict policies in place to act on.

- Never answer phone calls or read messages, e-mail, or comments sent by cyberbullies. Just set them aside in case they are needed by authorities as evidence or to take action. And instruct your kids to never answer a bully's calls or read their messages.

Many services enable you to block specific users. Check in the help files of the programs you or your child use to see how to do this. If you can't figure out how to block abusers, speak with your service provider directly. Finally, consider changing your e-mail address, cell phone number, user name, or password to avoid future communications. Online harassment is another good reason why you should not provide your contact information broadly and why you should use a separate e-mail or instant messaging account for online dating or socializing. (Most dating services provide you with a "blind" e-mail account for this purpose.)

Find Out More

Organizations such as WiredSafety (*www.wiredsafety.org*), Working to Halt Online Abuse (WHOA: *www.haltabuse.org*), and the Cyberbullying page of the Center for Safe and Responsible Internet Use (*http://cyberbully.org*), offer advice and are working to get federal legislation against cyberstalking in place.

PART THREE

Get Going to Protect Yourself Today

CHAPTER SEVENTEEN

Talking About Safety

In your everyday life, you have negotiated the levels of safety you practice with your family, with your neighbors, within your circle of friends, and in society, though perhaps not always consciously. Everyone in your family understands the need to lock the front door at night, why they shouldn't leave candles burning when nobody is around, and why the dog must be kept on a leash. All of these things help keep you, your family, and your neighbors safe.

Understanding the Safety Pacts You Make

The same logic behind your family's everyday safety practices can be applied when discussing and identifying safe Internet practices for you, your spouse, and your children, as well as the nature of your online interactions with friends, extended family members, and the public.

The level of safety people need or want differs from one person to another. Your rules are based on your personal and family values, your risk tolerance or risk aversion levels, how interested you are in reaching out to new people, and your age and the ages and maturity level of your children.

Your comfort level with technology also plays a role in how you create and enforce Internet protections. Technical experts will have a different perspective toward their online activities than someone who is technophobic.

When you think about your own comfort level from this perspective, you will probably find that your online safety needs mirror the level of safety you have established in the offline world.

Negotiating Safety

So how do you negotiate a safe online environment? You do it by reaching understanding and agreements with the people you interact with. The people you interact with most will probably be your family and close friends, but this negotiation extends to others as your online interactions expand.

Here are some ideas for how to approach the key people in your life to reach a consensus about online safety.

Negotiating with a Spouse or Partner

Information your spouse or partner puts online can have a direct impact on you. If they place your shared address, interests, vacation schedules, photos, and so on in the public domain—through online purchases, away messages on their e-mail, or blogging and/or social networking tools—you should negotiate and come to an understanding with your partner about this exposure so that you both feel protected and empowered to use the Web confidently.

Negotiating with Children and Teens

Safety isn't something you do *to* children; it is something you do *with and for* children and yourself. Safety is collaborative and takes everyone's participation to maintain. Rather than take a confrontational stance in "controlling" what children do online, consider treating Internet safety as a way in which the whole family supports each other. In this way, the discussion is a great deal like the way families agree that the last one out the door will always lock it.

Younger children and teens can endorse this approach to the Internet as well, as they already know that not everything online is good, and not everyone they meet online is their friend. Understand that kids can be very distressed by what they see and read online. Every year about 20 percent of young people receive an unwanted sexual solicitation, 25 percent receive unwanted exposure to sexual material, and many more are harassed, according to NCMEC. Kids don't want exposure to negative experiences any more than adults do. So explain that the family's goal is to create a defense against these unwanted encounters.

What You Should Know Before You Start the Discussion

Before you actually sit down to negotiate and discuss your family's strategy for Internet safety, it's a good idea to arm yourself with the information and experience you need in order to speak intelligently about the online world.

Getting Informed

As with every other aspect of life, having solid information on which to base choices is critical, but you don't have to be a "techspert" to take some basic online precautions. The chapters in Part Two of this book outline the most common areas of concern for individuals and families to think about. They describe potential risks and ways to mitigate these. Part Four includes a section on safety technology tools at your disposal.

Prepare with a personal knowledge of the technology products you own and services you subscribe to, combined with a clear sense of your family's personal safety needs and wants. Consider your sense of what is appropriate for your children, given your familiarity with their personalities, maturity levels, and ages. Include the awareness you've gained in reading the earlier chapters of this book, and you will have a solid foundation for a family discussion.

Experience the Internet Together

Beyond becoming informed, it's important that you experience the Internet with your family. Consider trying for yourself any online products that your children want to use, on any Internet-connected devices you have, so you have a deeper understanding of how they work.

For example: Learn to play games on Xbox and use the online interactive services; send text messages and try mobile chatting; set up a blog and play with the settings and options; try posting photos and text; and so on. Make your blog private and share it with only a couple of friends or your spouse, or make it public. Just think about what you are sharing and whom you should be sharing it with. Check out the blogs of others. You'll find out how useful and fun these services can be and see firsthand the ways in which people are exposing personal information. See how much information you can spot without using any technical aids, just from the content they've placed about themselves, the comments left on their blog, and what their friends are saying. You'll see how quickly this information can be stitched together, and your instincts for protecting yourself online will become fine-tuned.

> **Think About It**
> If using the Internet or mobile devices intimidates you, have your child teach you how to use the products and let them be the expert.

Build the Framework for a Safer Environment

It's useful to have a strategy for your implementation and ongoing guardianship of your family's online safety. There are three elements you can use to create a safer environment online or offline: educate, provide infrastructure, and enforce. This is like a three-legged stool that requires all the legs to support your safety.

Educate

It's important to have a frank and open discussion about both the benefits and potential risks involved in the use of online products, and refer to the chapters in Part Two of this book as needed. Cover both the potential for risks to your children and the potential risks to family or friends, keeping these points in mind:

- **Discuss how your children's friends might place them at risk.** (See more on negotiating safety with friends in Chapter 9, "Step 6: Reduce Your Vulnerability When Blogging.") Teach them that they have to look both ways when evaluating potential pitfalls because it is not only what they post, but what others might post about them or how others might use their information that can unintentionally place everyone in harm's way. Point out that publicly posted information is *searchable by anyone,* so the belief that no one will figure out their URL is very naïve. (Note: Some social networking sites have modified their policies so that minors' information will not be searchable, and you should require this of any service your child wants to use.)

- **Talk about cyberbullying and inappropriate contact by strangers.** Assure your children that they can come to you if there are any problems. Also make it clear that they themselves should never become bullies, as this is unacceptable behavior that can also be criminal. (See Chapter 16, "Step 13: Act to Avoid Harassment and Bullying," for more about online harassment.)

- **Teach kids how to make safe trade-offs.** For example, if your child wants to have a blog, walk through the choices available. Consider the safety and privacy policies of various sites, understand the level of protection they provide, and choose one that fits best with your personal views on safety. Identify those individuals your child wants to share information with, and then you can map that to what kind of information is appropriate to share. If they want to share only with close friends and family, they can share almost whatever they want without increasing their risk. Their friends already know what they look like, where you live, and how to contact your family. If they want to share their blog or social network with the public, you should help them understand what information is okay to make publicly available and what's not. Public blogs require that you provide more supervision, as it takes some training to really understand how people inadvertently leak their personal information.

- **Understand the exposure your profile gets.** Help kids understand that even if the public cannot see their blog without their (or your) permission, the public can often view their profile page. Help kids learn what information is okay to post publicly by asking this question: *If you wouldn't share the same information or images with a stranger who approached you for this information on the street, would you share it with potentially the creepiest person on the Internet?*

- **Understand that anything posted on the Internet can live forever.** All too many people have already had cause to regret some of what they've posted online. Don't post negative images of others. Consider how you would feel if that explicit or even suggestive image showed up in your grandmother's e-mail, on your wedding day, at your job interview, or at your college entrance board review. Be careful about what you enter in any forms. Did you answer "Yes" on the survey where it asked have you ever shoplifted? Did drugs? Stalked someone? Went to school/work drunk? Whether you answered seriously or not, that information, if publicly available, might come back to haunt you.

Provide Infrastructure

Examine what safety options you need to help protect everyone, and discuss how to build an environment for providing safety while allowing as much independence as appropriate. The need for infrastructure will vary from one family to another and from one child to another.

You might want to consider the following suggestions as you build your safety infrastructure:

- **Familiarize yourself with family-friendly safety software (often called parental controls).** Discuss the options within content filtering tools and what types of content you feel should be blocked or warned against. Set the content filters on your search engine to a level you are comfortable with. Look for solutions that allow *you* to define your content and safety preferences and not just ones that force a set of restrictions on you. The software and services you use need to be able to reflect your values and be easy to customize.

- **Agree upon the services and products that you will use.** Base this on children's ages and family values, and what safety settings you feel need to be in place. Should your child have limited feature access? Full access? Public or private access? Should parents manage the buddy list or review the list periodically? Should you check what's going on only if there's a problem? Have you created a safe environment so that your child feels comfortable notifying you of a problem?

- **Negotiate an agreement about the amount of time spent online, as well as specific amounts of time spent with different products and services.** This might be a combination of game console time, instant messaging time, computer time, and so on.

- **Just as with the TV, consider boundaries for Internet use.** For example, you might allow your children to be online before or after doing homework, and only until 9:00 p.m.

- **Evaluate where the computer and game console are placed in your home.** If they are kept in bedrooms, safety settings need to be a bit stronger because you will have less ability to view online interactions and usage.

- **Consider what cell phone features are appropriate.** This is especially important because there is little safety monitoring for these devices today, yet cell phones are becoming so advanced that they really are like portable and private personal computers. You might not want to purchase a cell phone for your child that has capabilities beyond your comfort zone to understand or adjust settings for.

- **Know what other access your child has to the Internet.** Find out what computer safeguards are utilized by your child's school and the public library, and at the homes of your child's friends.

Once you have held these discussions with your family, it's a good idea to have everybody sign on the dotted line by agreeing to a family contract. This documents what you've agreed to, and makes it easier to discuss situations that vary from the agreement because you already have a concensus about appropriate behavior. Figure 17-1 shows a sample family contract you can modify for your specific situation.

Internet Safety Contract for Families

The Internet is a public place, and I am responsible for using it safely.

☐ I will use only safe contact names (for e-mail, IM, on blogs, etc.).

☐ I will never use the Internet to bully or harass anyone.

☐ I will not post content to a publicly viewable site without my parents' permission.

☐ I will not expose my personal information, or information about my friends or family (name, address, phone or mobile number, school) in text or through pictures.

☐ I will never meet in person an Internet friend without telling my parents and having someone trusted with me.

☐ It is my responsibility to browse safely. I will not look for inappropriate content, and I will tell my parents if I see something that upsets me.

☐ I will download from the Internet only programs that my parents have approved.

☐ I will not register to use Web sites that require personal information, or take surveys/quizzes that ask for personal information.

☐ I know that information posted on the Web can live forever.

☐ I will think about who I am sharing information with and decide what is appropriate to share.

Child's name: _____ Date: _____

Figure 17-1 A sample family contract

Enforce

Establish the level of ongoing oversight and potential consequences if the family agreement is broken. Having clearly negotiated consequences can both help deter any urge to go around the system and make implementing the consequences less likely to cause an argument. Consider these suggestions:

- Set expectations that you will periodically review your children's Internet experience with them—and follow through.

- What happens if someone tries to circumvent the safety tools, tries to access a blocked site, surfs at inappropriate times, or spends too much time online? Define the consequences and make sure the whole family knows them so there are no surprises.

- What will be the consequences if you find out your child is being a cyberbully?

- What happens if your child's social networking site is exposing information that might place them, the family, or friends in harm's way? Do you forbid access? Does supervision increase? Do you pull back from a public to a more private setting? Only you can decide what is right for you and your family.

- How much oversight is enough to ensure safety, and at what point does that oversight become invasive? Again, the answers will be based on age, maturity, and family dynamics.

The Special Case for Social Networks

Social networks provide some rich opportunities to interact and participate with others every day—think of the great people you've met through friends and family members, and through friends of your friends and their family members. This networking approach to meeting new people and enriching your life has been a good social tool for millennia. You've probably relied on the good judgment of your friends whether it was to choose a hair stylist or business partner or to be introduced to a blind date.

Taking Social Networking Online

The ability to expand your social networks in the virtual world can mirror the benefits of networking in the real world, but there are a few risks to be aware of. In the real world, when you share information with your friends, it is primarily just between the people present at the time. If a record of what happened is kept, it's in someone's journal, or a story retold. In general, the distance that offline information travels is limited, as are the ways in which it can be documented. For example, rarely are photos added to a paper journal or diary; and when do others get to read a journal and vouch for its accuracy? Essentially never. For most people, most of the time, private information remains private.

It used to be that only celebrities and politicians had to be concerned about the risk of their private lives being made public. In the online world, your private information and actions can be documented and made public, often by you. Foolish indiscretions once shared with a select group now might be shared with the whole world. Things said in a context that was well understood at the time might take on an entirely different meaning to others. And to an extent never before imaginable, the information shared on the Internet has the potential for full multimedia support—text, images, video, audio, and corroborating documentation (others' comments that agree or comment on something)—documenting your words or actions forever. In a sense, everyone who participates in public social networks is suddenly a public figure. You should consider all the implications that status carries.

Taking Control of Your Blog

Here is a process you can use to help you and your family learn how publicly available blogs can put the family at risk. Follow these steps to teach your children how to blog safely:

1. Sit down and look at *other people's blogs* to find and highlight risky behavior based on what you've learned in this book. Talk about what is placing those people at risk. With this approach, the conversation isn't about your child doing something wrong. Instead it's about educating yourselves on how to spot and mitigate risks. This approach is considerably less emotionally loaded than using your child's blog as the "bad" example.

2. Once you've reviewed together other bloggers' mistakes, you might want to move directly to reviewing your child's blog, or you might choose to establish a short grace period, such as 3 to 24 hours, in which they get to clean up their site before you review it. If you do give them a grace period, let them know that all future reviews will happen on an ad hoc basis, at your discretion.

3. Assure them that the point of the review isn't to read every word written by them or to them. It's to ensure that their site isn't exposing information beyond the threshold your family has set. This is not just for the safety of the child who is blogging publicly. It is also to protect the entire family. If a cybercriminal knows your son's address, he also knows *yours*.

4. This safety review process can vary if your childen's blogs are private or if they agree to make them private after your talk. However, you should still review and discuss their buddy lists with them. If their buddy list includes people your child has never met, you should consider the blog public, requiring a more stringent review. The knowledge that a publicly viewable site will be regularly reviewed by parents might be a strong incentive for them to keep their blog private.

CHAPTER EIGHTEEN

It Takes Everyone to Make a Safe Internet

Think about the ways in which you try to protect yourself and others every day. You lock your doors. You don't talk to suspicious-looking strangers on the street, and you teach your children not to talk to strangers. You create neighborhood watches. If you see somebody being mugged or attacked, you call the police and find help for the victim. If a small child is standing at a crosswalk on a busy street, you might offer to help that child cross safely.

Being able to help others is part of what makes people civilized, and it feels good to make these connections with others. So how do you apply these social principles to become a good Net citizen? You learn how to help yourself, your family, and others to overcome the risks on the Internet. When you discover that you are not alone, that you have already learned basic safety skills in other parts of your life, that there is educational material to help you, and that you are part of an online community where people can support each other, you will begin to take charge of your online experience.

The majority of the online population is made up of good, well-intentioned people just like you. Learning to take safety precautions and working with each other, with Internet companies, with schools, with community groups, and with law enforcement will help make the Internet a safer place.

What to Do If a Sexual Predator Is Victimizing Your Child

Your 12-year-old child comes to you one evening after dinner with an anxious expression and blurts out that somebody he thought was an online friend has asked him to do something scary. You can tell he's uncomfortable, and he has probably made some kind of mistake he feels guilty about. You close the door, ask him to sit down, and think about what you should say next.

React Appropriately

Your first reaction at this moment should be to put yourself in your child's shoes and not be judgmental. Your child has come to you. This took both a lot of courage and a lot of trust that you would understand and help. Yet often many people's first reaction might be to say something like, "How could you have...?" This can violate a child's trust and make him feel you are blaming him. The likely consequence of that approach will be that he or she feels worse and won't come to you again. So, first you have to make sure your child feels supported and knows that you are on his side. Teaching safer behavior comes later. Right now you need to take appropriate actions to solve the existing problem and help your child.

Be sure to praise your child for having the courage to approach you so that together you can protect him and your family. If you discover the predator is a family member, it is especially important to support your child. Be absolutely sure you recognize that the person who has approached your child is the *predator*, and your child is the *victim*, no matter what kind of information or material your child has placed online.

This avoidance of blame is especially important because predators often work very hard to make the child feel guilty about whatever has happened. They do this to reduce the likelihood of the victim telling others about what's going on and to increase their victim's sense of being trapped in the abusive situation. Predators might use phrases such as "I only did this because I thought that's what you wanted" or "You wouldn't have come here if this isn't what you wanted" or "You shouldn't have made me angry."

Keep in mind that children (and adults) are often mentally manipulated and groomed for a considerable length of time *before* any physical abuse takes place. They might even have come to feel very dependent on the approval of the predator, or believe they are in a "love" relationship.

Ask the Right Questions

Begin by gathering information in a sensitive and understanding way. Who has contacted the child? What has that person asked of the child? What made the child feel uncomfortable? It is critical that you keep a level head and supportive attitude as you piece together an understanding of what has happened or is happening.

Report Abuse

Once you have determined that something inappropriate has happened, you need to take action. Immediately stop any avenue of contact your child has with the predator, and take steps to report the problem to the appropriate authorities.

Why People Don't Report Abuse

There are many reasons why people of any age don't report abuse. The abuse might have been too traumatic for them to deal with; they might distrust the authorities; they might be afraid of reprisals to themselves or other family members. It might be a family member who was the abuser. Parents might feel that they and their child have already been through enough and are not strong enough to face a long, drawn-out legal battle, or they simply want to keep their family out of the headlines or courts.

For whatever reason, people often opt to simply try to block the predator from any contact and potential for harm and leave it at that. Only the individual or family can weigh the factors and make this call, and should you find yourself in this situation, you might well want to consider getting counseling or advice about your choices. This should be available as a free service through crisis centers, a school counselor, or your pediatrician.

> **Find Out More**
>
> You can also contact the National Center for Missing & Exploited Children (NCMEC) at *www.missingkids.com* for advice, information, and to report abuse.

Why You Should Report Abuses

Only you and your child can decide the right course of action. But when abuse is not reported, you leave the predator loose on the Internet and streets where they are likely to do the same things to countless other families, whether their abuse is harassment, fraud, or sexual in nature.

Think About It

Data from the NCMEC (National Center for Missing & Exploited Children) indicates that in the United States 25 percent of girls and 20 percent of boys are sexually exploited before they are 18. This means that sexual abuse is a preventable disease that strikes 22 percent of our children. It cripples their bodies, their minds, and their souls. This scourge is not an Internet phenomenon, but the Internet is a powerful tool used by predators to find and abuse new victims.

Reporting Abuse You Observe

You might also witness abuse of others online. For example, you might observe harassing behavior in a chat room or in an instant messaging exchange with your friends. This is a tricky situation because it's not your family that's involved, and you aren't familiar with nor do you control the values of the family of the person who is involved in the harassment.

If you know the person involved, say, it's a friend of your child, talking with that child or phoning the parents might be appropriate. If you or your child witness harassment of somebody you don't know, you could consider reporting this to the online provider. Chances are, if an individual is acting inappropriately, others have reported the problem, and your report will help your provider and/or law enforcement to discipline or prosecute the person.

Also, you can report inappropriate or illegal images, hate speech, or other violations of your rights, the rights of others, or the site's privacy codes to the hosting site.

Where to Report Abuse

If you or someone in your family has been the victim of online abuse, either through a financial scam, fraud, or harassment of some type, what do you do? Once you've made the decision to report the abuse, how do you go about it? There are several options, depending on the situation. In the United States you can

- Report the incident to your Internet or wireless phone service provider. Get more information on the specific Web service's site; for example, on MSN's Online Safety & Security page at *http://safety.msn.com*.

- Take any consumer complaint about fraud to the U.S. Federal Trade Commission (FTC) or get advice on how to recognize or avoid rip-offs at *www.ftc.gov/ftc/consumer.htm*.

- File a complaint with the Better Business Bureau if you are the victim of an online scam. Go to *www.bbb.org* for more information.

- Report Internet fraud to the FBI through the Internet Fraud Complaint Center at *www.ic3.gov*.

- Report abuse of a child to the National Center for Missing & Exploited Children (NCMEC) at *www.missingkids.com/cybertip/*.

  In countries other than the United States, check online or with your local police force to find out how best to get the help and support you need.

- Whenever you feel a crime has been committed, contact your local police. They can investigate or put you in touch with other agencies as appropriate. If the cybercriminal is from another country, you should still contact your police department, which can contact additional law enforcement agencies as necessary.

> **Think About It**
>
> If you know about a child who is in immediate risk or danger, call local law enforcement. If you have any information about a missing child, call 1-800-THE-LOST (1-800-843-5678).

Find Support After Your Report

Don't forget to take care of yourself and your family after reporting abuse. After the anxiety of worrying about your loved one, as well as the stress of finding your way through the reporting process, you might all need support.

You need to know you are not alone. You can contact local crisis centers for 24-hour telephone assistance. Or visit the Web sites of the following organizations to get information and support for victims of online abuse, as well as additional reporting resources:

- The world's largest online safety and help group is WiredSafety (*www.wiredsafety.org*). They have information about reporting abuse through their Cyber911 Tiplines and live online help.

- The International Centre for Missing & Exploited Children (*www.icmec.org*) and the National Center for Missing & Exploited Children (*www.missingkids.com*) provide information on resources that can help if a child is being sexually exploited.

- SafeKids.com (*www.safekids.com*) offers an online safety quiz and kids' rules for online safety that might help you in educating your family.

- At BlogSafety.com (*www.blogsafety.com*) you can visit the CyberTipline to report abuse that takes place on your blog.

Additional sites worth visiting are

- *www.safeteens.com*

- *www.staysafe.org* has sections for kids, teens, parents, and teachers

- *www.getnetwise.org*

- *http://kids.getnetwise.org/safetyguide*

- *http://safety.msn.com/*

- *www.microsoft.com/athome/security/default.mspx*

- *www.microsoft.com/mscorp/safety/default.mspx*

Find Out More

Be sure to check out "Helpful Web Resources for Internet Safety" in Part Four of this book for more helpful Web sites related to safety online.

What Your Online Service Can Do

Your online service provider's site has privacy policies and codes of conduct that describe appropriate behavior and the ways in which they protect members and their privacy. They can expel an offender from their service for inappropriate behavior or, in more severe cases, contact law enforcement and cooperate with them to prosecute a criminal who has committed a crime using their service.

Your provider should offer you

- Clear safety messaging and instructions on the proper use of their products

- Easy-to-find advice and information about how to respond to abuse; ideally, abuse reporting information should be on every page of their site

- A way to easily report abuse to them, if you choose to do so

- Safety settings so that you can help manage the level of exposure you or your family receives online

- Fast response to an abuse report

- Confidentiality

- Strong ties to law enforcement so that predators and criminals can be caught and punished

How You Can Affect Laws Dealing with Online Abuse

You have the opportunity to be part of the changing legal landscape regarding Internet and wireless communications. The first thing to do is to educate yourself about potential risks online. This book gives you a good start. Now you should go out and learn about existing legislation. Visit *www.whitehouse.gov/omb/legislative/sap/109-1/hr3132sap-h.pdf* to read the Children's Safety Act of 2005 and how it applies to online sexual predators, for example. To check out currently pending legislation in the House of Representatives, go to *www.house.gov/house/Legproc.shtml.* Write to your political representatives and let your voice be heard.

Find Out More

Check your state attorney general's Web site for information about pending state legislation involving online safety.

You can also contribute your time and energy to various groups working to inform and track legislation. The Get Involved page of the National Center for Missing & Exploited Children (*www.missingkids. com/missingkids/servlet/PageServlet?LanguageCountry=en_US&PageId=245*), WiredSafety's Volunteer page (*www.wiredsafety.org/volunteer/*) and NCH's site (*www.nch.org.uk/getinvolved/*) suggest several good ways to make a difference in your community.

Begin a New Internet Journey

By now you might feel a little overwhelmed. You might have been "hit" by scams, snarled in spam, harassed by Internet road ragers, carjacked by criminals, or just offended by content you'd rather not have seen. Perhaps you never considered that you'd better *look both ways* before going online, nor stopped to teach yourself or your family how to navigate the Internet safely.

Hopefully, this book has been useful in providing a sense of confidence so you can use great products and services comfortably, and reject products that do not meet your safety demands. Perhaps you've gained some insight about how to experience all the Web has to offer—*on your terms*.

The Web will continue to change as new products and services are developed and refined. As it does, simply remember these guidelines:

- Consider what you share, and with whom you share it.

- Look not only at what opportunities products make possible, but also at how they might be used by a potential predator.

- Understand the motivation of sites and other users you interact with.

- If a deal sounds to good to be true, it probably is.

If you follow these simple guidelines, you'll have significantly decreased your risks.

Many of you might still have questions, and I will try to answer them through my Web site, *www.look-both-ways.com*. This is a free, public service site dedicated to helping individuals navigate the Web safely. Questions and answers are posted on the Web site so that you can search through what others have asked and learn more.

I also post additional safety information on the site: examples for you to practice with, templates you might want to use, and articles on topics covered in this book and on new technologies. Refer back to the site whenever you have a question and to get information on new technologies and how to use them safely.

PART FOUR

Resources

Helpful Terms

adware A form of malicious code that displays unsolicited advertising on your computer.

antivirus software Computer software that attempts to block malicious programs/code/software (called viruses or malware) from harming your computer.

blog A diary or personal journal kept on a Web site, usually updated frequently, that might be private or might be intended for public viewing.

bots Computer programs that automatically perform a repetitive task, such as searching through Web sites or indexing information.

buddies (buddy list) A list of friends you interact with online through various media such as instant messaging.

buddy search When two (or more) Internet users search the Web together, both users see the search results simultaneously.

chat room An online site used for social interaction, usually based on a topic or theme, where people with shared interests can meet others.

content filtering Allows you to block certain types of content from being displayed. There are certain Web sites that you know you don't want your children to see. Many software programs allow you to block information that you find inappropriate or offensive. Some of the things you can screen for include coarse language, nudity, sex, and violence. In addition, many Internet browsers have parental controls to help protect your child from stumbling onto inappropriate sites. You can often choose separate levels of security for each child based on their ages and maturity levels.

cybercriminals   Those who commit criminal activity that targets computers or information or that leverages computers and online information to find real-world victims.

cybersex   Also called "computer sex," "Net sex," and "hot chat." Refers to virtual sex encounters in which two or more persons pretend to be having actual sex through describing their actions and responding to their partner's descriptions. This is mostly done through text, images, voice, and video.

discussion boards   Also called Internet forums, message boards, and bulletin boards. These are online sites that allow users to post comments on a particular topic.

download   Transferring material from a server or remote computer to your computer, mobile device, or game console.

e-mail signature   A block of text added at the end of an e-mail message, usually automatically. It can contain your full name, your job description, location, or phone number, and even an inspirational thought.

emoticons   Small graphics (like smiley faces) used to indicate emotional state, opinion, or response when no body language is providing those cues.

file sharing   The ability to store files either in a central place that can be shared with as few as one other person or publicly. Files can be stored on the Internet or on any computer that provides access to others. File sharing allows others who have permission to access the shared file to modify or download it.

firewall   A security system usually made up of hardware and software used to block hackers, viruses, and other malicious threats to your computer through a network such as the Internet. Installing or activating a firewall feature on your home computer is one of the most important actions you can take to help to protect your computer.

for-pay items (winks, avatars)   Low-cost add-on products that allow users to customize their experiences on cell phones or in instant messaging devices. These can be cartoon-like images (called avatars) or animated cartoons (called winks) that you can send to others.

game console   A machine that is specifically designed for playing video games (although it might also play movies), often hooked up to a TV or computer monitor for viewing. Not all game consoles are capable of Internet connections or are connected to the Internet, but if they are connected they allow users to play games with others remotely.

gamer tag   The nickname a user has chosen to be identified by when playing Internet games.

gaming   The act of playing or participating in online games.

grooming   The systematic way that sexual predators manipulate their victims into trusting them, depending on them, and ultimately meeting them. This usually involves sympathy, subtle ways to alienate the victim from others, and flattery. It might also involve money, gifts, or promises of work—especially "modeling jobs." Predators are very skilled at tuning into whatever tactics will work with a particular child given their specific vulnerabilities, and adapt their strategies accordingly. This might occur over only a few days, or might happen over an extended period of time, often between one and six months of slow "seduction." Often older children are so mentally manipulated that they actually come to believe it is a "love" relationship and might willingly participate in their own abuse. It might take years for them to realize the exploitive nature of the abuse.

GSM (Global System for Mobile communication)   A digital cellular telephone technology. This system is used mainly in Europe, Australia, and the Middle East, although it is becoming more popular in the United States.

handle   (as in "blog handle") A nickname an Internet user chooses to display to others online.

identity theft   Stealing someone's identity in order to impersonate them, usually for financial gain.

instant messaging   A real-time, text-based communication used on desktop computers, cell phones, and other devices to send short messages between individuals.

interactive gaming   The ability to play games online, interacting with other players. Covers a broad spectrum of activities from children's games to online gambling.

keystroke logging A legitimate way for software developers to understand what is happening as they write code. It can also be used to track a user's activities online to either monitor or spy on (depending on your point of view) what they type and what sites they visit. A keystroke-logging program might be downloaded by parents to watch their children, by children to watch their parents, or by one adult to watch another adult. It might also be downloaded onto your computer in stealth by malicious cybercriminals who then have information about your online activities sent to them so that they learn your passwords and banking information, for example.

location application A program that enables you to locate the whereabouts of anybody logged on to the Internet from a variety of devices.

malware Stands for malicious software; an umbrella term that includes any type of harmful code—Trojans, worms, spyware, adware, and so on—that infiltrates a computer without the consent of the computer user and is designed to damage the computer, collect information, or allow the computer to be subverted and used remotely to send spam.

Multimedia Messaging Service (MMS) A method for sending messages from mobile phones that includes audio, video, or images.

mobile computing Use of a portable device that provides computer functions and can usually connect to the Internet, even when changing locations.

parental controls Products or services that offer options to parents to help restrict their child's experiences with media or filter media content. These restrictions are currently applied to television services, computer and video games, and Internet access.

peer-to-peer A method of sharing files directly over the Internet from one Internet-enabled device to another (computer, mobile phone, and so on). This is often done with music files, for example, which might violate copyright laws if the people involved make copies of the material without permission to do so.

persona The person an Internet user chooses to appear to be, rather than the person they are. For example, a 56-year-old man might assume the persona of a 12-year-old girl who wants to meet other 12-year-old girls.

personal digital assistant (PDA)   A small handheld computing device typically used to track appointments, contacts, and e-mail.

phishing   The practice of scamming someone into divulging confidential information they normally would not provide to a stranger. The lure is typically via e-mail that brings the user to a scam Web site. The purpose of phishing is to gather the information needed to steal a victim's money or identity.

posting information   To upload information to the Web.

predator   Anyone who preys on others.

remote access   The ability to allow access to your computer by another user at another location. Remote access is often used in technical support as a way to fix problems, as it provides full access to the information stored on the computer through a data link.

scam   To con, cheat, trick, swindle, sting, or rip off others.

search engine   An Internet service that helps you search for information on the Web.

smartphone   A handheld device that incorporates features of a mobile phone, with PDA functions such as a calendar or contact database. Smartphones allow you to install additional features on them.

SMS   Stands for Short Message Service, a form of text messaging on cell phones, sometimes used between computers and cell phones.

social networking   A category of Internet applications to help connect friends, business partners, or other individuals together using a variety of tools.

spam   Unsolicited e-mail attempting to sell you something. Also known as junk mail.

spim   Spam sent via an instant message, typically unsolicited and attempting to sell you something.

splog   Spam sent via blogs, typically unsolicited and attempting to sell you something.

spyware   Software that collects information about you without your knowledge or consent and sends it back to whomever wrote the spyware program. Spyware might look for your banking information, personal information, and so on. It is illegal and pervasive.

Subscriber Identity Module (SIM)   A small card that holds your identity, authentication, address book, and so on, in some cellular phones.

surfing   Similar to channel surfing on a television, Internet surfing involves users browsing around various Web sites following whatever interests them.

text messaging   A method of sending short messages (also called SMSes, txts, or texting) between mobile phones, other computing devices, and even some landline phones.

URL   Uniform Resource Locator, a unique Internet address of a file or destination. To find a particular site or document, type the URL into the browser window and the browser will bring up that particular Web site.

user name   The name a user selects to be identified by, for example on a computer on a network or in an online gaming forum (also called nickname or gamer tag).

videocams   Also called webcams. Video cameras that are often (though not always) attached to a computer so that a video image can be sent to another when communicating online.

virus   A self-replicating software program that spreads to other computers by sending copies of itself to other devices hidden in code or attached to documents. Viruses are often deliberately destructive to any device that becomes "infected," often destroying data or disabling the device's operating system.

Voice over Internet Protocol (VoIP)   Use of an Internet protocol to transmit voice communications. VoIP allows you to hold voice conversations over the Internet.

Web hosting   A service that provides individuals, organizations, and businesses with online storage space to store and share information, images, blogs, video, or any other content accessible through the Web.

Technology Toolkit

Protecting yourself online takes two kinds of safety. This book is dedicated to helping you learn how to modify your behavior online. The second kind of safety comes from using all the protections technology has to offer. As mentioned up front in this book, this section is intended to provide only an overview of the safety technologies you should be using. There are many resources available to you if you need a deeper understanding of the excellent technology tools that can help you to

- Cut down on the amount of unsolicited information you receive

- Set parameters for the online content you deem appropriate for your kids

- Defend against malicious technology attacks in the form of viruses, spyware, and other malware (any *malicious software* that includes a variety of nasty code designed to harm your computer or steal your information)

These programs are usually very effective, and there is every reason to take full advantage of their benefits.

Understanding the Types of Technology Available

There are certain fundamental security products and services that everyone should be using. I recommend that you take advantage of the following:

- **Operating system and other software updates.** Every operating system gets updated when people discover possible ways to exploit it. Getting these updates (commonly referred to as "patches" or "security patches") onto your computer is critical; they ensure that you have the latest features and any fixes to security issues that have surfaced since the product was installed or last updated. If you are using Microsoft Windows as your operating system, you should set up your computer to automatically check for, and download, the latest updates. If your computer uses another operating system, learn how to obtain such security updates from the software help system or documentation.

- **Firewalls.** A firewall puts restrictions on what information can come through to your computer. Don't use the Internet without one. Depending on the settings you choose, a firewall will reject unsolicited requests coming to your computer over the Internet, or will check with you about whether to block or allow such requests. This helps to cut down on the number of viruses and/or other malware that can affect your hard drive. Microsoft Windows provides a big dose of protection with its built-in firewall setting. Other firewall programs are also available, such as ZoneAlarm and Norton Personal Firewall.

- **Antivirus software.** It's critical that you install an antivirus program, such as those from McAfee, Symantec, or Trend Micro, or the antivirus protection included with security suites such as Windows Live OneCare. AVG Anti-Virus Free Edition is one of a few free antivirus programs. There are two important things to remember about this type of program. First, you must frequently update the virus definitions in them to deal with the latest viruses. Second, be sure to run a scan of your computer frequently. The good news is that you can set up these programs to automatically download updates and scan your computer for viruses at set times, for example, once a day late at night when it won't interfere with your use of the computer.

- **Anti-spyware/anti-adware software.** With the amount of spyware and adware attempting to download to your computer at any given time, this is also a must-have security tool. There are several good free anti-spyware/adware programs available, such as Windows Defender (which you can download from *www.microsoft.com/athome/security/spyware/software*), HijackThis 1.99.1, and Lavasoft Ad-Aware SE Personal Edition 1.06. However, in order to get *automatic updates*, you might need to purchase a subscription.

The alternative is to frequently check and update the service manually. If you manually update, it is critical that you do so frequently because cybercriminals move quickly to the next method of attack when they realize that anti-spyware/adware software has begun to block their existing method.

Note: The tools just listed are available either as standalone applications, or in bundled suites such as Windows OneCare or Norton Internet Security. Suites typically offer you a better price compared with buying each of the applications separately.

- **Browser settings.** Your Internet browser should help you moderate your Internet experience, but in order to do so, you need to tell it what settings match your values. Look for settings, such as the Internet Options in Internet Explorer, that you can set for privacy and content you want to allow (see the following figure), and what you want your browser to block. **Note:** Browser settings alone provide only a measure of content filtering. To comprehensively filter content, you need filtering software as well.

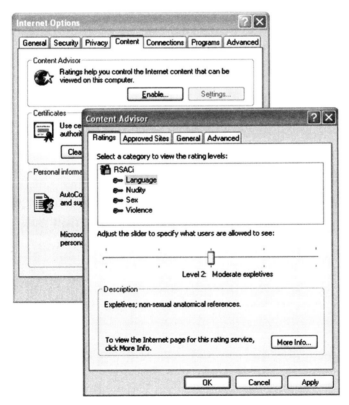

- **Parental controls or Family Safety.** Many ISPs and Web portals provide safety settings (often called parental controls) that you can use to limit or monitor your children's activities online. I'm proud to say that Microsoft is taking the lead in this area by providing Windows Live OneCare Family Safety *free of charge* to help users manage their personal interactions and those of their families. The Family Safety beta program will be available beginning in the fall of 2006. To learn more about Windows Live OneCare, go to *http:// onecare.live.com*. You can also search online for other products that provide various levels of monitoring.

- **Filtering software.** Filtering software helps you set boundaries for the types of images, sites, and content that your family is exposed to. You can use programs such as Windows Live OneCare Family Safety (mentioned previously), Net Nanny, ContentProtect, and CYBERsitter to manage Web surfing results and to filter news-groups, chats, peer-to-peer access, pop-ups, and more. Depending on the product, filtering software can provide reports or e-mail alerts about what sites your children have tried to access. Filtering software can work by using keywords you set, such as "sex" or "vio-lence," by checking for specific URLs you choose to restrict access to, or by implementing more advanced technologies that analyze objects on sites. To learn more about Microsoft's free-of-charge filter-ing software, go to *http://onecare.live.com*; you can also search online for products that provide various levels of monitoring.

- **Image-editing software.** Before posting a photo online that is avail-able to the public, you might want to remove or disguise any infor-mation that would expose your identity or location. You can use a basic program such as Windows Paint to make simple changes, such as placing a black box over somebody's eyes to obscure their face. Many graphics programs, such as Microsoft Digital Image Suite, Corel's CorelDraw, and Adobe Photoshop, come with image-blurring capabilities, which is a slightly more sophisticated way of distorting an element in a picture rather than simply blacking it out.

Top Tips on Using Technology to Protect Yourself

How you use a product can be as important as what product you use. Here's my best advice on how to fit technology tools into your plan for Internet safety:

- **Understand what your family is comfortable with.** Before you begin to experiment with the various programs and settings that are available to help protect you online, keep in mind that tools enable you *to create the online environment you feel is appropriate*. These programs typically offer various levels of settings. For example, a high level of content filtering would restrict a large number of sites, while a low level would allow more types of content through. Before you begin to make settings and install software, talk to your family and consider what the trade-offs are. If you leave your settings at the lower level of filtering, less "good" material will be blocked, but potentially more "bad" material might get through. How will you adjust your settings and standards as you and your children age? Being thoughtful about which tools you use and how you use them will have an impact on how rewarding and appropriate your online experience is. To help guide you in age-appropriate Internet usage, Microsoft has partnered with the American Association of Pediatrics to provide a guide to recommended levels of filtering by age group. To learn more about the AAP guidelines, go to *www.aap.org/healthtopics/mediause.cfm*.

- **Understand the capabilities of your mobile phone and of your child's mobile phone.** Talk to your carrier about what safety measures they have enabled. Consider the services available to you and your children and enable only the ones you feel are appropriate. More advanced phones can now be infected with malware. Talk with your cellular company about what risks might be associated with your phone and what you should do to protect your devices from viruses and spyware. For the youngest users (7- to 12-year-olds), limited-functionality phones, such as Firefly and those from Disney Mobile, have been launched in some markets. These phones provide restricted contacts, fewer buttons, and full parental controls.

- **Look for advanced filtering features.** Check to see if your filtering program will route e-mail alerts to you when your child tries to access a restricted site and needs your permission. If you travel for your job, you might want to look for a product that offers remote reporting and management. With these features, you can check on what's happening at home from anywhere in the world and even change configuration settings remotely. Some products offer a dynamic filtering feature that allows site access when the content is not objectionable (for example, a news site that changes its feature articles throughout the day) and blocks it when there is objectionable content.

Useful Web Sites for Finding Tools

Here are some useful Web sites to help you track down the best software protection tools.

Products

- Windows Defender, *www.microsoft.com/athome/security/spyware/software/default.mspx*
- Windows Live OneCare, *http://onecare.live.com*
- Norton AntiVirus and Personal Firewall, *www.symantec.com*
- McAfee VirusScan, *www.mcafee.com*
- Trend Micro PC-cillin Internet Security, *www.trendmicro.com*
- Net Nanny, *www.netnanny.com*
- CYBERsitter, *www.cybersitter.com*
- Lavasoft Ad-Aware, *www.lavasoft.com*

General Information

- About.com information on antivirus software, *http://antivirus.about.com*
- Review of 2006 antivirus software products, *http://anti-virus-software-review.toptenreviews.com/?ttreng=1&ttrkey=antivirus+software*

- Review of 2006 anti-spyware software products, *http://anti-spyware-review.toptenreviews.com*

Find Out More

If you are interested in learning more about Microsoft's security products, visit *www.microsoft.com/security/default.mspx.*

Helpful Web Resources for Internet Safety

The following list provides useful links maintained by organizations and governments in various countries to help you educate yourself about online safety, and report abuse when you encounter it.

Safety Advice and Information

www.look-both-ways.com   The site maintained by the author of this book to provide information and helpful links on Internet safety.

http://safety.msn.com   Microsoft's Internet service, MSN, provides online safety information on this site.

www.microsoft.com/athome/security/default.mspx   Microsoft's Security At Home Web page with advice on using family contracts and more.

www.microsoft.com/mscorp/safety/default.mspx   Microsoft's Safety Web site with information about phishing, safety legislation, and more.

http://staysafe.org   An educational site about safety and security issues online.

www.wiredkids.com   A nonprofit site dedicated to protecting children from sexual exploitation online.

www.wiredsafety.org   A U.S. nonprofit touted as the "world's biggest online safety and help group."

www.icmec.org   The International Centre for Missing & Exploited Children's site offers features for information and activism.

www.cox.com/TakeCharge A safety information page from Cox Communications, an Internet/TV/cellular phone service provider.

www.stalking-research.org.uk/index.php This site lists ages of online harassment victims posted by Cyberstalking Information (CSI).

www.safechild.org A site dedicated to preventing online bullying and emotional and sexual abuse.

www.blogsafety.com A discussion site operated by nonprofit TechParenting Group based in California.

www.getnetwise.org Get information on spam, hackers, viruses, identity theft, and more.

www.wiredsafety.org/volunteer If you want to get involved, check out WiredSafety's Volunteer page here.

www.nch.org.uk/getinvolved This is the NCH's official Web site.

http://www.familysafemedia.com/pornography_statistics.html This page of the Family Safe Media Web site presents statistics on kids' exposure to online pornography.

http://www.microsoft.com/windowsxp/using/games/getstarted/esrbratings.mspx Check here for a guide to using ESRB ratings.

http://www.mailfrontier.com/forms/msft_iq_test.html This is one of a number of great Web sites where you can learn more about phishing and even test your skill at spotting fakes.

www.stoptextbully.com The NCH maintains a Web site that offers great advice about dealing with cyberbullying.

www.haltabuse.org Get involved in stopping online abuse at this site for the organization Working to Halt Online Abuse (WHOA).

http://cyberbully.org The Cyberbully page of the Center for Safe and Responsible Internet Use.

Recognizing Sexual Predators

http://beachildshero.com/traits.htm A nonprofit organization that provides an outline of sexual predators' behavior and recommends possible prevention and deterrence strategies.

http://voicelessvictims.org/2005/11/psychological_profile_of_a_chi.php
Voiceless Victims is dedicated to providing a forum for victims of crimes and exploitation, and has a section on the profile of predators.

www.csom.org/pubs/mythsfacts.html A project run by the U.S. Department of Justice in the Center for Sex Offender Management that outlines myths and facts about sex offenders.

www.cfc-efc.ca/docs/mnet/00001239.htm Child & Family Canada is maintained by a consortium of 50 Canadian nonprofit organizations dedicated to providing resources on children and families, and includes a profile of online predators, how to safeguard your children, and what to do if they are being targeted.

www.familywatchdog.us/Search.asp In addition to providing a resource for safety overall, Family Watchdog provides Americans the ability to find if there are predators living in their neighborhood, or to find where a specific predator is residing by entering their name.

www.mako.org.au/prelist.html MAKO provides a sex offender registry for Australia. (Australia is the only country other than the United States with a system for locating sexual predators.)

Government Sites

www.whitehouse.gov/omb/legislative/sap/109-1/hr3132sap-h.pdf The U.S. president's Statement of Administration Policy regarding the Children's Safety Act of 2005.

www.house.gov/house/Legproc.shtml The United States House of Representatives site listing legislation before Congress.

www.ftc.gov/bcp/conline/edcams/kidzprivacy/index.html A site focused on kids, parents, and teachers with resources and information on online safety.

www.ftc.gov/ftc/consumer.htm The Federal Trade Commission site you can access for help with online financial scams.

www.fbi.gov/publications/pguide/pguidee.htm The FBI's guide to online safety for parents.

www.ncjrs.gov/internetsafety/children.html The National Criminal Justice Reference Service site's page on Internet safety for kids.

www.ftc.gov/bcp/conline/edcams/infosecurity   This FTC site includes information on consumer, business, and kids' concerns with online safety.

www.missingkids.com/missingkids/servlet/PageServlet?LanguageCountry= en_US&PageId=245   The Get Involved page of the National Center for Missing & Exploited Children.

www.sec.gov/investor/pubs/askquestions.htm   Look here for a detailed list of questions you should ask before investing online.

www.consumer.gov/idtheft   Visit FTC's Identity Theft Web site at this address for steps you should take if you are a victim.

www.netalert.net.au/02531-Advice-Centre.asp   NetAlert's Web site. NetAlert is an Australian nonprofit organization established by the government to provide advice about Internet access.

Sites for Reporting Abuse

www.missingkids.com   National Center for Missing & Exploited Children.

www.bbb.org   The Better Business Bureau's Web site where you can report online abuses by companies.

www.cybertipline.org   A site of the National Center for Missing & Exploited Children that gathers leads on instances of sexual abuse.

www.ic3.gov   The Internet Crime Complaint Center sponsored by the FBI and NW3C.

http://inhope.org/en/index.html   The International Association of Internet Hotlines (INHOPE) is a European Union–supported organization with 23 member hotlines in 21 countries that responds to reports of illegal content to make the Internet safer.

Kid-Oriented Sites

http://kids.ninemsn.com.au/article.aspx?id=18301   NineMSN is a joint venture between Microsoft's MSN and Australia's communication company PBL. This page offers a safety resource center and lots of kid-friendly features such as Hi-5 and New MacDonald's Farm.

http://staysafe.org   An educational site about safety and security issues online.

www.kidsmart.org.uk   An award-winning Internet safety site geared toward schools, kids, and parents.

www.stoptextbully.com   A site of NCH that tells kids how to stop people who are text bullying them.

www.childnet-int.org/youngpeople   Childnet International's site with features such as online role-playing and case studies of online abuse of children.

www.netsmartz.org   The NetSmartz Workshop is an interactive, educational safety resource from the National Center for Missing & Exploited Children (NCMEC) and Boys & Girls Clubs of America (BGCA) to teach kids and teens how to stay safer on the Internet.

www.safeteens.com   A sister site to BlogSafety, this site offers advice to teens and parents.

www.teenangels.org   A division of WiredSafety.org run entirely by teens trained by law enforcement to run programs for teens on online safety.

Common Messaging Shortcuts

Having trouble understanding text messages from your teens? Here's a short, fun guide to decoding text messages (Dcodng txt msgs).

2DAY   today
2Hot2Hndle   too hot to handle
2MORO   tomorrow
2NITE   tonight
4EVRYRS   forever yours
4get   forget

A

A/S/L   age/sex/location
AAM   as a matter of fact
AB   ah bless!
ADctd2Luv   addicted to love
AFAIK   as far as I know
AKA   also known as
ALIWanIsU   all I want is you
ALOrO   all or nothing
ASAP   as soon as possible
ATB   all the best

B

B4   before
BaBitsU   baby it's you
BBFN   bye bye for now
BBSD   be back soon darling
BCNU   be seeing you
BdBy   bad boy
BF   boy friend

BFN   bye for now
BGWM   be gentle with me (please)
BRB   be right back
BTW   by the way
BYKT   but you knew that

C

Cld9?   cloud 9?
CMIIW   correct me if I'm wrong
Crzy   crazy
CSThnknAU   can't stop thinking
      about you
CU   see you
CUIMD   see you in my dreams
CUL8R   see you later
CYA   see ya

D

D8   date
DIKU   do I know you?
DLTBBB   don't let the bed bugs bite
DuUWnt2GoOut2nite?   do you want
      to go out tonight?

E

EOL   end of lecture

F

F2F   face to face
F2T   free to talk
FITB   fill in the blank
FWIW   for what it's worth
FYEO   for your eyes only
FYI   for your information

G

GAO   glad all over
GF   girl friend
GG   good game
GMeSumLuvin   gimme some lovin'
GMTA   great minds think alike
Gr8   great
GrOvyBab   groovy baby
GrwOldWivMe   grow old with me
GSOH   good salary, own home
GSOH   good sense of humor
Gtng2gther   getting together
GTSY   glad to see you

H

H&K   hug and kiss
H8   hate
HAGN   have a good night
HAND   have a nice day
HITULThtILuvU?   have I told you
    lately that I love you?
HldMeClse   hold me close
Hot4U   hot for you
HTH   hope this helps

I

IAC   in any case
ICLW\YLuv   I can't live without
    your love
IDK   I don't know
IDntDsrveU   I don't deserve you
IGotUBbe   I got you babe
IIRC   if I recall correctly

IJC2SalLuvU   I just called to say I
    love you
ILU   I love you
ILUVU   I love you
IMBLuv   it must be love
IMHO   in my humble opinion
IMNSHO   in my not so humble
    opinion
ImRdy4Luv   I'm ready for love
ImT14U   I'm the one for you
IOW   in other words
IOWAN2BWU   I only want to be
    with you
IPN   I'm posting naked
IWALU   I will always love you
IYKWIM   If you know what I mean
IYSS   if you say so

J

JM2p   just my two pennies' worth
JstCLMe   just call me

K

KIT   keep in touch
KOTC   kiss on the cheek
KOTL   kiss on the lips

L

L8   late
L8R   later
LETA   letter
LMAO   laughing my ass off
LOL   laugh out loud
LstinU   lost in you
LTNC   long time no see
LTR   long-term relationship
LtsGt2gthr   let's get together
Luv2LuvUBab   love to love you baby
LuvisTDrug   love is the drug
LuvMeLuvMyDog   love me, love
    my dog
LuvU   love you

M

M$ULkeCraZ   miss you like crazy
MBURBMJ   my but you're beautiful
    Miss Jones
MGB   may God bless
MkeMyDaSa+!   make my day, say yes
MMDP   make my day punk!
MO   moment
Mob   mobile
MYOB   mind your own business

N

NE   any
NE1   anyone
NIFOC   naked in front of computer
NO1   no one
NP   nosy parents

O

OIC   oh, I see
OLL   online love
OTOH   on the other hand

P

P911   my parents are coming!
PA   parent alert
PAL   parents are listening
PANB   parents are nearby
PCM   please call me
PLS   please
PM   private message
POS   parent over shoulder
PPL   people

Q

Q?   question?
QT   cutie

R

R   are
ResQMe   rescue me
RMB   ring my bell

RmbaYaMne   remember you're mine
ROTFL   roll on the floor laughing
RU?   are you?
RUOK?   are you okay?

S

Salt&ILDoIT   say it and I'll do it
SETE   smiling ear to ear
SIT   stay in touch
SITD   still in the dark
SO   significant other
SOH   sense of humor
SOHF   sense of humor failure
SOME1   someone
SRy   sorry
StckOnU   stuck on you
StndByYaMan   stand by your man
SvnALMyLuv4U   saving all my love
    for you
SWALK   sent with a loving kiss
SWG   scientific wild guess
SYS   see you soon

T

TAW   teachers are watching
TDTU   totally devoted to you
THNQ   thank you
Thx   thanks
Ti2GO   time to go
TIC   tongue in cheek
TkeAChnceOnMe?   take a chance
    on me?
TLMeImDrmn   tell me I'm dreaming
TMB   text me back
TMIY   take me I'm yours
TPTB   the powers that be
TTFN   ta ta for now
TTYL8R   talk to you later
TWIMC   to whom it may concern

U

U   you
U+Me=Luv   you + me = love

UCnDoMgic   you can do magic
UdoSumthn2Me   you do something
   to me
UR   you are

W

WAN2   want to
WAN2TLK?   want to talk?
WenCnICUAgn?   when can I see you
   again?
WER R U?   where are you?
WLUMRyMe?   will you marry me?

WRT   with respect to
WTGP   want to go private
WTTW   word to the wise
WUWH   wish you were here

XYZ

X   kiss
Xclusvly Yas   exclusively yours
XLNT   excellent
Xoxoxoxo   hugs and kisses
Y?   why?
YBS   you'll be sorry

Selected References

Finkelhor, D., K. J. Mitchell, and J. Wolak. 2000. Online Victimization: A Report on the Nation's Youth. NCMEC.

Huffaker, David A. and Sandra L. Calvert. 2005. Gender, Identity, and Language Use in Teenage Blogs. *Journal of Computer-Mediated Communication*, 10 (2), article 1.

Lanning, Kenneth V. 2001. *Child Molesters: A Behavioral Analysis, Fourth Edition.* NCMEC.

Wolak, J., D. Finkelhor, and K. J. Mitchell. 2004. Internet-initiated Sex Crimes against Minors: Implications for Prevention Based on Findings from a National Study. *Journal of Adolescent Health*, 35 (5), 424–433.

Wolak, J., K. J. Mitchell, and D. Finkelhor. 2003. Internet Sex Crimes against Minors: The Response of Law Enforcement. Alexandria, VA: NCMEC.

Index

About the Authors

Linda Criddle is an active mother of four and a 13-year Microsoft Corp. veteran. As senior product manager for child safety, she works on developing child safety strategy for MSN and Windows Live, participates in Microsoft-wide child safety planning, identifies emerging risks to adults and children on the Internet, drives the MSN and Windows Live abuse prevention and monitoring strategy, helps develop safety messaging within MSN and Windows Live Products, and creates safety solutions for end users and technologies. Linda lectures and advises on Internet child safety risks internationally. She also trains product teams, and speaks about Internet child safety at conferences and universities, and for school districts, parent groups, teens, and law enforcement. Linda has codeveloped more than 30 patents on Internet safety and emerging technologies for Microsoft. Prior to her current position, Linda worked for MSN as a product planner. In that role, she worked on the company's vision for mobile services and helped define new features for MSN Mobile services releases and represented Microsoft at mobile Internet safety conferences internationally. Since joining Microsoft, Linda has also worked with Microsoft's Consumer Products Group, worked on the development of Microsoft's internal e-commerce tools, and was a senior financial analyst for the Office Division. Linda grew up in California, and then lived and worked in Kristiansand, Norway, for 15 years before joining Microsoft. In Norway, she was active in city politics and a member of the Kristiansand City Council. During that time she served as vice chair of the council's environmental committee and sat on committees for tourism and education. She also has a background in investigative journalism, and has covered business, economic, and political issues. Linda lives in the Seattle area.

Nancy Muir is the author of over 50 books on technology and the Internet (some under the name Nancy Stevenson), including *Distance Learning Online For Dummies* (Wiley Publishing, Inc.) and *10 Minute Guide to Motivating People* (Alpha Books). She recently won a Benjamin Franklin first place award for her book *Young Person's Character Education Handbook* (JIST Publishing, Inc.) from the Independent Book Publishers Association. Nancy has taught technical writing at the university level and, prior to her freelance writing career, worked as a manager in both the book publishing and software industries.

What do you think of this book? We want to hear from you!

Do you have a few minutes to participate in a brief online survey? Microsoft is interested in hearing your feedback about this publication so that we can continually improve our books and learning resources for you.

To participate in our survey, please visit:
www.microsoft.com/learning/booksurvey

And enter this book's ISBN, 0-7536-2347-3. As a thank-you to survey participants in the United States and Canada, each month we'll randomly select five respondents to win one of five $100 gift certificates from a leading online merchant.* At the conclusion of the survey, you can enter the drawing by providing your e-mail address, which will be used for prize notification *only.*

Thanks in advance for your input. Your opinion counts!

Sincerely,

Microsoft Learning

Microsoft | Learning

Learn More. Go Further.

To see special offers on Microsoft Learning products for developers, IT professionals, and home and office users, visit: *www.microsoft.com/learning/booksurvey*